What Money Really Means

●

Thomas M. Kostigen

ALLWORTH PRESS
NEW YORK

For My Mother

07 06 05 04 03   6 5 4 3 2

Published by Allworth Press
An imprint of Allworth Communications
10 East 23rd Street, New York, NY 10010

Cover design by Douglas Design Associates, New York, NY

Page composition/typography by Integra Software Services, Pondicherry, India

Back-cover Photo courtesy Scott Thun

ISBN: 1-58115-259-0

LIBRARY OF CONGRESS CATALOGING-IN-PUBLICATION DATA:
Kostigen, Thomas. Waht money really means/Thomas Kostigen. p. cm
Includes index. ISBN 1-58115-259-0 1. Money. I. Title.
HG221 .K743 2003 332.4–dc21 2002004403

Printed in Canada

Contents

Section 3: The Spiritual Attachment of Money:
What Money Should Mean

Preface

There is a "mini me" inside me; He's in my head. He's thinking other thoughts when I'm listening to someone speak. He's contemplating my next move when I'm playing a game. He's the one always trying to change me. He's who I'll be when ... He's full of proposition, while I'm this somewhat stagnant being. He will become the person I hope to be: full, complete.

What He needs is the means to do all the things He wants. If He had this amount of money, He could do that. If He had that amount of money, He could do this. Then, of course, once He gets this or that, He—I—will change. We'll be *perceived* differently. We'll *be* different. We'll be that person He always thought of, that person we ought to be, if only ...

There are a lot of "if onlys" these days. There's a New Economy, $100 million lottery winners, an even a widely watched television show that asks, Who Wants to be a Millionaire? I think I do. I know He does. In fact, I wonder why I'm not like the thousands of millionaires branded last year. Or like the seven million millionaires out there in the world today. What do they have that I don't (besides the money, that is)?

If we had that much money would it really change us? Would we really think differently, act differently, develop new friends and relationships? Would it make us happy—He and I—one, fulfilled?

Okay, so these aren't easy questions. We'll have to find people who might provide some insight on what it's like to have always had money, to just get money, to get money and lose it, or to never have money at all.

He is, of course, already imagining some of these people. From the Dalai Lama to dot.com billionaires, from the Rockefellers to indigents. He is at once envisioning incense and robes, beads and introspection, and at the same time picturing Ferraris and champagne, mansions and private jets. A back alley. People picking out of a garbage can.

The dichotomies He imagines are extreme. But that's what He is there for. I, on the other hand, have to live in the here and now. So, it sure would be nice if we could get together, He and I.

This inquisition is, perhaps, more about that than what money means. For money holds the freedom of the self; it allows us to act out our imaginations, be whom we've always dreamed of being. But what happens to the imagination then? Where does He go once His visions are realized? And what will happen to the self—me, that is? Would I just become what He has imagined? Would I live my life in snippets of the style displayed in magazine ads, films, television commercials? All these things that money could buy. A new life? A new lifestyle? Would those "if only" feelings of inferiority just pass? What new feelings would arise?

I'll turn to some people for insight. He'll envision what they mean. And maybe—just maybe—between us we'll create some understanding.

●

The Physical Manifestation of Money and Attachment: What Money Is

CHAPTER 1

The History of Money

1 EUR = 0.9463 USD, 1 USD = 105.39 JPY, 1 CHF = 0.06466 EUR,
1 GBP = 1.506 USD, 1 CAD = 0.7145 EUR, 1 JPY = 0.01 EUR,
1 CAD = 0.6758 USD

We've all seen this equation, posted at banks, airports, on the Internet. This currency equation is a deeply meaningful barometer of value. It defines costs, and tells you that if you spent a dollar on a cup of coffee in the United States, you're going to have to spend one hundred and five yen for a cup of coffee in Japan. But price is a far thing from worth. And worth may be a far thing from value.

To understand what money means we have to understand worth and value: those things money is supposed to represent.

My Imagination sees a man crawling onto an oasis from the desert—sunburned, exhausted, his clothes tattered. Would he pay more for a glass of water than someone not suffering from thirst? Of course he would. Hence, the value. Hence, what it's worth. But what would he pay with? If it's money, then money means survival. It means the ability to live. Once the man's thirst is quenched, the worth of water to him would decline. It would get poured into a nominal value system. That's when things get complicated. The value of money has to be assessed. For in and of itself, money is nothing more than paper and coins. Without value, a jingle jangle, origami is about all money would be good for.

So, what exactly is money and where did it come from? Adam valued fruit, but he didn't have to pay for it (with money that is). In the beginning, there wasn't any money. And that should tell us something. Like all inventions, time included, money is defined by the people who made it up, concocted the idea. Money is a conception. From it, a whole value system has been created. And

— 3 —

that's not just economics. That value system often defines our social status, our professional lives, our leisure abilities, our relationships, and most of all our purchasing power. In other words, it defines us in a way.

So, what great ape set these definitions? Who defined money?

The word "money" stems from the Latin. It derives from the Roman goddess Moneta. Moneta is another name for Juno, the Roman goddess of heaven. She, the wife of Jupiter, is also the goddess of light, birth, women and marriage—some of those things that give meaning to life, that *mint* us to one another.

The Romans played an integral part in devising money and its value. However, the actual conceivers of money were the people of Lydia, an ancient city in Asia Minor, or modern-day Turkey. Money was first minted there in the seventh century B.C.

Lydia began to mint coins made of electrum, which is a mixture of gold and silver. The government issued these bean-shaped ingots and marked them with their weight and value in lieu of pieces of gold and silver, which had been the standard barter material because of their scarcity.

Lydia was part of the thriving society of Asia Minor at the time. There, where the first trade centers of the world evolved, discoverers and inventors created an attractive marketplace. Commerce soon exploded—and the government of Lydia minted money to control the way in which things were bought and sold. With government-minted money, they could control price and value; that is, worth.

Governments, ever seeking control, could now exercise their influence on commerce. Needless to say, the "money" idea caught on. And before long, most of the governments of the world were issuing some semblance of coinage. But, 'round about the first century A.D., the Roman government overindulged and minted too many coins. It had needed the money to build and finance its military. Inflation occurred—and the value of money became an issue. To make up for the loss in value of one coin, people obviously had to carry more coins. Hauling around buckets of coins wasn't particularly convenient for the horseback, mule-riding, pedestrian society of the Middle Ages. So money-lenders and merchants began to issue promissory notes in lieu of coins. Ah, huh, another breakthrough in the creation of money. Someone was on to something, and credit currency began to be widely used as a system for buying and selling. Indeed, even today if you look at a dollar bill, you'll see that it's a promissory note "For All Debts Public And Private" issued by the government.

My Imagination is at it again, trying to conceive of things we haven't experienced. He tries to envision life without money, life in situational barters. How would it change? How would it differ? We would still have to utilize skill—whatever skill we had—merely to subsist or obtain objects of value to pay for our subsistence. What would we do for trade? I don't think there would have been a market for writers, mostly because there were no books. I would have had some very simple choices: craftsman, consul, farmer, butcher. My place in society would then have been set. I could trade on that value. With that value, I could acquire the things or barter the things I would need to survive, like shelter. My Imagination sees: a horse, a cow, a pelt, a good spear. Those bartering objects that have utilitarian value. What a jump it is to representative value. All those barrels full of coins. The use of gold and silver as the basis for value because they were scarce in supply, creating a relatively stable value system, until that day in Rome when perhaps on a hot summer morning a man in toga and sandals pushing a wheelbarrow full of coins stops to wipe his brow in front of, say, the Colosseum and gets an idea for paper money. "A bit lighter on the back and feet," he might have thought, looking up at Palatine Hill.

Paper money was used by private lenders and merchants for centuries until France, in the eighteenth century, formally standardized the use of government issued notes, or "paper money."

This was quite a controversy at the time. Paper money meant governments no longer had to use gold or silver in the minting process. They could create value with a printing press, albeit they had to physically back the paper with reserves of gold.

The United States and money became indelibly entwined when the dollar took on the indicia of the United States: $. In fact, worldwide the standard base currency became the U.S. dollar after World War II. Still, though, its value was tied to gold.

In the early 1970s, almost a hundred years since its inception, the United States was in economic turmoil. The value of the dollar had plummeted, and inflation was doing what it infers: going up. That made the dollar worth less gold. And Fort Knox would have been barren if dollars had been traded for bullion; there wasn't enough gold reserve to cover the "value" of U.S. currency.

A lot of people were focused on what money meant in the 1960s and 1970s. Money meant capitalism, it meant world influence, or hegemony. And it became *the* philosophical schism of the for the Cold War—between a nation state devoted to communism, where all people would ideally share in each other's riches, and a nation state whose basis was steeped in capitalism.

Money's influence to embark on the Vietnam War, to quell the philosophy of the anti-money movement of the time, sent the world into disarray. Oil prices and other commodity prices surged. Money became less valuable. Its relative worth to gold was plummeting.

While all this was going on in the world, the banking industry was working on a concept that would forever change the monetary value system and its tie to any physical denomination.

In 1958, Bank of America issued sixty thousand credit cards to the residents of Fresno, California. These credit cards represented value—but not in the form of paper or coin. Plastic was introduced into the repertoire of physical representatives of money. This was further elaborated upon when Dee Hock, the founder of VISA, developed a system where value would become "data" in the form of electronic particles able to move around the world at the speed of light. Money had become an idea represented in digits. It was slowly losing its link to gold and physical or tangible value.

In 1971, President Richard M. Nixon cut the link. He abolished the gold standard. A new system of global exchange rates was established—and paper money around the world lost its link to a tangible asset. No more gold. No more silver. Currency would represent nothing more than devised value. Its power would be in its potential.

Now, people were in control of the value of money. By setting lending rates and gauging the growth or slow down of productivity of a nation, people could increase or decrease the value of money around the world. Indeed, by 1976 the Articles of Agreement of the International Monetary Fund had been amended to legitimize the practice of letting currencies fluctuate. Until then, fixed rates had been agreed on between nations (shortly after World War II at the Bretton Woods Conference in 1944).

With "people" now deciding what things are worth, money has become a disembodied principle of value, of worth, of purchasing power. These people who decide how much purchasing power it's going to take to buy that cup of coffee, who set rates of exchange, who determine "value," are economists, money managers, traders, and financial analysts.

Unlike their predecessors, the new breed of money manager doesn't deal with paper or coin. The new breed of money manager deals with digits, numerals on a computer screen. Money is a series of representations. We read or are told what these representations mean. And, voilà, that is money, that is what money is worth.

Even paper and coins are being replaced more and more by the representative plastic card. The credit currency of the past is the credit card of today. There is less attachment to the physical "money" used to buy, sell, or value material goods. Indeed, I have gone days without using any physical money. With a debit card or a credit card, I can purchase just about anything I need. My bank account is automatically debited money for goods and services; nothing changes hands. It's all a blip on a screen. Those blips, those digits, are what money managers oversee, analyze—and try to make sense of.

The idea of money is what has become all important. It's the idea of having it, not particularly seeing it, that drives my Imagination, for example. He doesn't need to see it to conceive of utilizing its purchasing power. Money, to Him, doesn't need to be fetched, transported, and exchanged for goods or services; the purchasing power of money is communicated.

The evolution of money has transgressed the physical and has found itself anew in a global compositional equation. Money provides the ability to do certain things. It holds that proposition. It is full of "if onlys."

Money to the Lydians meant control. It meant creating a basic system of value. It meant creating some type of comparability among goods and services. By doing that, the Lydians spun the world away from utilitarianism and toward an interpretational matrix of worth.

Money to the Romans meant power and influence. It meant imperialism through a well-financed military. Money could buy power. It could buy control. It was the capture of power and control—through disparate ideologies—that decidedly split the world into two superpowers. It was the exorbitant financing of a military that led to the downfall of the Soviet Union and its communist economy.

President Nixon's lifting of the gold standard meant that money could stand on its own. Dee Hock's disorderly abstract placement of value on goods and services meant money, in its tangible form, could disappear. To him, to financiers, and other professional money managers, money means a system for the exchange of value. This system, made up of blips of electronic digits, has created more wealth over the last ten years than in the course of history.

The value proposition money holds has been exploited to the tune of some seven million millionaires, five hundred billionaires, and a generally expanding world economic environment. The value of money is strong. It's a New Economy. Just as those electron digits travel at the speed of light, so too is wealth created and lost today. The digits that represent our "value," our "worth," are housed by an account, identified by a number. The digits are influenced by the monetary system—and their value, our value, is thus determined.

My Imagination can't see money anymore. He sees a blurry, gray computer screen displaying digits. But it doesn't mean much to Him. Dollars, however, bring a flash of excitement. He sees the green and white notes—the $1 bill with the face of George Washington; the $5 bill with the face of Abraham Lincoln; the $10 bill with the face of Alexander Hamilton; the $20 bill with the face of Andrew Jackson; the $50 bill with the face of Ulysses S. Grant; and the $100 bill with the face of Benjamin Franklin. Those dollars mean something to my Imagination. They service the spirit. They hold the potential of being fulfilled.

My Imagination sees a teenage Lydian boy tossing a coin high in the air and catching it as he strolls. He sees the young Lydian in knee-high sandals, a simple tunic, curly brown hair. It's a summer's day. The boy smiles as he looks at the ingot; he is going to use it to buy a gift for his girlfriend, or so my Imagination decides. The Lydian will buy a locket and present it as they lie by the side of a river. She will be twirling a golden flower—perhaps a chrysanthemum—and drop it after he has given her the locket. They will kiss, rise, hold hands, and skip off down the riverbank. The plucked chrysanthemum will remain in the grass where they lay. It will lie tilted, its stem angled toward the ground. She had meant to present the young Lydian with the flower. She had wanted to present it to him as a sign of her love. She hadn't purchased it; she had simply plucked it from the garden behind her house just before he had come to greet her.

Dialogue: Me and My Imagination

"So that's the story of money."

"The history."

"And where does that leave us?"

"Past the beginning."

"True. But to be honest, I've already imagined what money is. I want to imagine what it's like to have it."

"And do what?"

"Anything. That's the terrific thing. We'll be free to do what we want."

"So you're imagining that once you get enough money, you can do what you want? I think that's naïve."

"Enlighten me."

"I hope to. But first, I think we have a few gaps in our foundation."

"I'm picturing a house."

"Not that. Our story. Money is—what? We know how it came about. But we have yet to hear what money really is."

"Bills, coins?"

"That's currency."

"Give me something to work with."

"I can't. That's what's missing. We haven't explored worth. We haven't explored value. We've only uncovered how a simple coin came to represent these things."

"And how do you propose to explain that? Value and worth aren't imaginable to me. The coin is. I can't see abstract concepts. I can't equate symbols to those things. I need things, things that can represent other things. But I need things nonetheless."

"How about instead of things, I give you someone."

"I'll take what I can get."

CHAPTER 2

The Mechanics of Money

It's fall in Connecticut. The leaves are changing. Students are strolling the streets of New Haven, their backpacks filled with books. I can see my breath in the air.

I've pulled up to a rambling, old New England mansion in a mild state of disrepair—broken shutters, peeling paint. The grass needs cutting. I pay the taxi driver and walk to the front door, where I'm greeted by a maid. She tells me to wait in the breezeway while she goes to see if the professor is ready to see me.

I'm here in New Haven to interview Martin Shubik, the Seymour Knox Professor of Mathematical Economics at Yale University. Professor Shubik is widely considered an expert on money, its history, and what it means.

I meet Professor Shubik in his study in the rear of his house. It's book filled, of course. The wood floors need refinishing. His desk runs in an L-shape to give him room for a computer (the only discernible modern item in the room). The desk is essentially two large pieces of wood propped on a sawhorse.

Professor Shubik himself is the human embodiment of his house. He even does a few quick fix-its as we speak—cleans his ears, his teeth.

National Public Radio is broadcast (loudly) from an old hi-fi. I'm fearful I'll be recording an account of the plight of the Nambalese gorilla (yes, I made that up) instead of Professor Shubik's insights on money. But thankfully my recorder comes through. I'll say that again—thankfully my recorder comes through—because Professor Shubik goes into quantum physics to describe money and what it means. And I'm not kidding.

Professor Shubik says that money is based on two things: trust and information. These concepts aren't static. Therefore, traditional theories explaining money like the "equilibrium theory" are wrong. Rather, it's quantum theory that holds true.

Stick with me here. I know it may get a little "thick," but it all makes sense in the end.

"In classical equilibrium theory in economics, agents submit their demand-versus-price functions to a 'central agent,' who then determines the relative prices of goods and their allocation to individual agents. The absolute prices are not fixed, so the process does not determine the value of money, which merely enters as a fictitious quantity that facilitates the calculation of equilibrium. Thus, traditional equilibrium theory does not offer a fundamental explanation of money, perhaps the most essential quantity in a modern economy."

My Imagination is stifled. My mind is unwinding the words, equating meaning, processing. There isn't room for images, never mind a story or tangent on which to affix. Professor Shubik, I think, senses when the left side of the brain needs a little help from the right side. It must have been all those years of teaching. So he tells me a story about sardines:

"This story really contains the essence of what money is about.

"An importer imports a whole bunch of sardines. He sells them to a distributor. The distributor sells them to some wholesalers. The wholesalers sell them to some retailers. The retailers sell them to customers. The customers complain bitterly that they've been poisoned, and this feeds all the way up the chain and reaches the importer. And the following conversation takes place between the importer and the main distributor:

"'I've called up to complain about the sardines.'

"'What was wrong with the sardines? Didn't you sell them to the other distributors?'

"'Yes, I sold them to the distributors.'

"'Did you get your 30 percent?'

"'Yes, I got my 30 percent.'

"'So what are you complaining about? What did the distributors do?'

"'The distributors sold them to the retailers?'

"'Did they get their usual markup?'

"'Yes, they got their usual markup.'

"'And what did they do?'

"'The retailers sold them to customers.'

"'Did they get their usual markup?'

"'Yes.'

"'So what are you complaining about?'

"'But, the customers came back and wanted to kill the retailers because they claim they were buying tainted sardines.'

"There was a silence on the phone. And finally the importer comes back on the line and says, 'We are trading sardines, not eating sardines.'"

I get the sense that this is intellectual humor, so I chuckle. I'm not exactly sure of where Professor Shubik is taking me with all this. Thankfully he explains the story:

"That's the original premise in which the formal existence of money came into being—that they were trading sardines. Therefore, the original means of payment were barley or silver or gold. It could have been anything. Then things became a little more sophisticated and coinage came into being. The coinage was a just a manufacturing process, but a manufacturing process taken over by the government. And the customary something off the top was about 3 percent. But what did they give you for the 3 percent? They gave you a guarantee of quality, a guarantee of standardization, and a legal system. Now trade took off and what you had was the general acceptance of the legal system, coinage and what have you. But then underneath it, slowly it dawned that as long as sardines are accepted in trade and as long as no one tries to eat them—the boxes could be empty."

The point, you see, of Professor Shubik's story is "the boxes could be empty." Money itself, he says, has three basic qualities: storage of value, means of payment, and *numeraire*. These add up to the constructs of money.

"Numeraire has to do with measure. It's the measuring sticks, the measurement system you use. You use money to measure value. But the numeraire property is such that it doesn't mean that there's got to be a physical existence of the actual item. Means of payment merely says well, I will accept the stuff. Well, why will I accept the stuff? That's the tricky thing," says Professor Shubik.

Why will someone value something at X rather than Y? Here is where trust, information and quantum physics all merge.

"The Nambalese gorilla is an indigenous herbivore of the Northern African plains where English hunters sought to exploit their rare pelts for trade . . . "

My Imagination corners a gorilla peeling back the skin of a banana. He is seated at a desk in a classroom. He takes a bite of the banana and cocks his head to one side as he reads the chalkboard.

$$\sum_n ({}^p/_n {}^q/_n - {}^p/_n + 1{}^q/_n + 1) = 0$$

Professor Shubik is standing in front of the chalkboard holding a pointer. He's explaining that it's the variables, like conditions and time, that determine value and give money its meaning.

"The correct way to approach the understanding of money and financial institutions is pure physics," he says.

I snap out of it. I no longer see him in front of the gorilla, nor in a classroom.

Professor Shubik leans forward at his desk in his study and reproaches me for not knowing the determinant values of money. He chastises me for not knowing the philosophy of David Ricardo. But I bear him out and wait for him to settle into the rest of his discussion. I figure he must have caught me daydreaming.

Value. Professor Shubik is stuck on the point of value in our discussion. It's the value that is conditional. And that, at the end of the day, is all that money is. Money itself is an amoeba; it can take on many forms to equate value to goods or services. It's conditional, and its only construct is the faith and trust and belief in it.

Professor Shubik explains that originally money had an equitable value, in the form of gold, silver, or some other replacement item. But, as governments "got into the act," as he says, replacement value became mythical.

Gold coinage or silver coinage is one thing, but as soon as the world moved into paper currency, the concept of money took a new direction.

"The way you hook the public into something like that is you have a myth which says that they [notes] are redeemable in gold. Therefore there is a mysterious place like the vaults of the Bank of England or Fort Knox which has enough gold to pay every one off in real value. But that gold is trading sardines. There is nothing," Professor Shubik says.

Okay, okay, I too get the point. Professor Shubik is saying that in an orderly society, you don't need the gold, or the commodity. It's the trust of a government's backing that is the thing. You could use paper, cigarettes, a pair of socks. The thing you use to represent value doesn't matter, as long as the government backs it. The problem is who to trust: gold or a politician? That's Ricardo's line.

Back to the session. We go through money's history, some trivia. Finally, I can tell that the professor is winding up his dissertation. He stands and walks about the room. He gets some heat going in his body, which is wrapped in a sweater and scarf. He tells me that he has been sick and almost died twice over the past two weeks. Professor Shubik is very old.

His last points he makes carefully. That there is a subtle distinction between credit and money, as money has lost its tie to anything "physical." That the offset for money—as guaranteed by governments—is pain or death.

This gets my interest. I reel in my Imagination, who is starting to wonder about the professor's condition. Instead, I give my full attention to this financial scholar

"Essentially what the state produced was: 'We guarantee that this is what this coin is made of and if it turns out that somebody has mucked around with it, we'll kill him,' which was the standard penalty for counterfeiting," says Professor Shubik. The guarantee is guaranteed by that penalty, death.

Today, it's different but not dissimilar. It's not death that is threatened, it's bankruptcy.

Now instead of gold or coins, we have an abstract symbol. "And we invent a measurement and the measurement is called the dollar. Now, do we have an intrinsic value for the dollar? Now strange as it may seem, implicit in the economic system there really is a utilitarian intrinsic value for the dollar, but it's negative. What I mean by that is the value for the dollar is somewhat determined by the default in bankruptcy laws in society. How unpleasant does it get for you when you go broke for an imaginary buck? So that gives it a value. It's a negative value, and it ties it into the credit system. The dollar is a mythical commodity invented by the government. You and I can't get away with that, but the government can," posits Professor Shubik.

He is getting tired, I notice. It takes him longer to get out a sentence. There are long pauses between words.

"Money," he says, "is information, reputation and trust."

His final explanation is of networks.

"Trust and information is what a governmental monetary system is about. At a more complex level the whole financial system and banking system is the transformation of small networks where the players are unknown into bigger networks that are known and the words are known and trusted and respected," he says. "For example, I, Martin Shubik, cannot get a stranger to take my IOU note. So, how do I get a stranger to sell me something? I go to a god damn bank who's got a prime name because they're known by a few million people and have got a reputation. I exchange my IOU note for the bank's note and I pay the individual with the bank's IOU note. And the individual may take the bank's IOU note and convert it into so-called cash money, which is the United States' IOU note: dollar bills. But the IOU notes are such for the United States that they never have to pay them.

"Government money is a purely dynamic concept. The purely dynamic concept is this: that you can get a system of exchange going where everybody knows that the paper is of no value in terms of eating. But as long as everyone believes that everyone else is willing to accept it, then everyone will accept it. Hence, it's pure information."

Speaking of information, I'm on overload. So, we quickly wrap things up. Besides, the professor is tired.

I exit the same way I came.

" . . . and the Nambalese gorilla is nearly extinct . . . "

The taxi retrieves me from in front of Professor Shubik's home. When I pay the driver, I think of what those bills mean—a magnificent signifier of trust. I board the train and exchange another set of bills for a ticket. The conductor wakes the man I sit next to and asks him for a ticket. The man explains that he has already paid; he can't find his receipt. No matter, the conductor knows him. He trusts what the man says and moves on down the aisle, punching little holes in small pieces of paper marking where we've been and where we're going.

I wonder if I were to relay the same information as the man did, would the conductor believe me? Would he trust what I had to say?

Dialogue: Me and My Imagination

"So money relies on me at the end of the day."

"Seems so."

"Trust and information. You have to imagine those things. You can't hold them in your hands."

"But you can't picture them either. You have to impose reason. So, it's a paradox."

"I can't imagine something, and you can't physically value something without imagining it."

"Even if you could it wouldn't mean anything. It's what we believe to be true, what we put trust and faith in that creates value, makes something worth something, or worth something else."

"Paper and coins."

"Or nothing."

"I can't imagine that."

"Sure you can. Paper and coins are old hat. Debit cards. Credit cards. That's currency."

"I can imagine those things."

"You may just be imagining the cards themselves, not what they represent. That's data."

"Money as data? You're right. I can't imagine that. But I can imagine that chips could store data—whatever that looks like—and those chips could be worth something."

"But we're not talking about a physical symbol here. Data are made of electrons and photons. Energy."

"Help! Please help! It's fine for you to process this, but I can't imagine anything but the uses of this data. On their own, data are information. They can be packaged in any number of different ways."

"And that information is conditional. And that information changes. It varies."

"So how do values stay constant? Where do data bridge the gap?"

"It does seem rather mind-bending. In fact, the person who created money out of data is an interesting enough fellow. Perhaps we should ask him."

CHAPTER 3

The Evolution of Money to Data

I had geared up for the challenge. I'd read his book, combed through his articles. Most recently, I had tried to attend a conference his organization was hosting—to no avail. I finally got through, however. I finally booked my time with Dee Hock, the founder of VISA. What was to be a scheduled ten-minute discussion turned out to be an hour's talk about everything from the biosphere to biomechanics. All of this, I should note, was in the context of money—what it means, how everything relates to everything else in the planet, on this one and the next, and then next, until the whole universe can be accounted for, right here, right now, in this space, in this time we are spending together.

Dee Hock, somehow I need to call him Mr. Hock, founded VISA in the 1960s. He took a simple concept of a bank-issuing credit card company and took it global. The concept, I came to find out, was not so simple. In fact, it changed the way that money is handled. Mr. Hock made money of 1s and 0s. He decimalized value and made it part of a string of electrons in a computer.

To give you some idea of the weight of our discussion, let me explain how VISA was begun. Better yet, let me allow Mr. Hock to explain how VISA was begun.

"Are you sure?"

"Yes."

"But it's your book."

"Yes, yes, that's true. But VISA was your concept. Go on. Really. I'd rather."

"Okay, if you say so . . . Can you hear me in the back? Good."

My Imagination wants Mr. Hock and me to trade places in this discussion. Mostly because he doesn't trust me, my Imagination. He likes Mr. Hock's words, his thoughts and ideas better than my scribbling, my raconteur. So be it. I, the physical self, will give way to my Imagination and Mr. Hock.

"It was necessary to reconceive, in the most fundamental sense, the concepts of bank money and credit card, and to understand how those elements might evolve in a micro-electronic environment."

If I scan a dollar bill on to a computer screen, is it still a dollar bill?

"What is it that we want to accomplish? How will we organize it?"

A Palm Pilot.

"Money had become nothing but alphanumeric data recorded on valueless paper and metal. It would become data in the form of arranged electrons and photons that would move around the world at the speed of light, at minuscule cost, by infinitely diverse paths, throughout the entire electromagnetic spectrum. The concept of 'credit card' was inadequate. Credit cards had to be reconceived as a device for the exchange of monetary value in the form of arranged electronic particles. Demand for that exchange would be lifelong and global, twenty-four hours a day, seven days a week, wherever the customer happened to be. Perceptions swiftly changed."

There's a light show at the Museum of Science in Cambridge, Massachusetts. In a dark, circular room, people stand. Blue lights, red lights, green lights flash in sequences to music. Fast then slow. Slow then fast. They walk outside the room. The show continues. They're left in wonder. How can they keep hold of that magnificent sensory world?

"Embedded in what had seemed a hopeless problem was an incredible opportunity. Any organization that could globally guarantee and clear monetary information in the form of arranged electronic particles in every monetary value in the world would have the market—every exchange of monetary value in the world—that staggered the imagination. But a major problem remained."

Could they box the light show, keep it in their left pocket?

"No bank could do it. No stock corporation could do it. No nation-state could do it. In fact, no existing form of organization could do it. It would require a transcendental organization linking together in wholly new ways an unimaginable complex of diverse financial institutions, individual customers, merchants, communication companies, suppliers, and government entities. It was beyond the power of reason or the reach of the imagination to design such an organization or to anticipate the problems and opportunities it would face.

"Evolution routinely creates complex organizational patterns—rain forests, marine systems, body, brain, immune systems. If anything imaginable were possible, if there were no constraints whatever, what would be the nature of an ideal organization based on biological organizing principles to create the world's premiere system for the exchange of monetary value? VISA was born of that idea."

If the light show was in my left pocket—

Okay, okay. I, the real self, am taking back control from my Imagination.

My research finds that VISA is a nonstock, for-profit membership corporation. It is an inside-out holding company in that it doesn't hold but is held by its functioning parts. The institutions that create its products are, at the same time, its owners, its members, its customers, its subjects and its superiors. And it isn't subject to any regulatory authority in the world. It transcends language, custom, politics, and culture and connects more than twenty-one thousand financial institutions, sixteen million merchants, and eight hundred million people in three hundred countries. Its annual volume exceeds $1.5 trillion per year. And its only has a staff of three thousand.

The importance of the VISA story in my discussion with Mr. Hock is that its evolution, essentially, mirrors the concept of money. Indeed, it is the concept of money. All the principles that hold true for money hold true for VISA.

"Money is information," Mr. Hock says. "But then there is the question of value. At the heart of VISA was an understanding."

It was the understanding among banks that VISA would be honored that created value.

"Money had really become nothing but alphanumeric information," Mr. Hock says. "There had to be the belief that someone would accept it."

The idea that banks were behind VISA provided the concept with value. That concept became money. It became a belief system that empowered people to trade value without the need for physical numeraire. Storage of value and means of exchange were all that would be needed to allow value to escape into the world, sneak out without its clothes on, and be invisible to the human eye.

"It's a range of electrons and photons that move at the speed of light and bounce around the universe," says Mr. Hock.

What is the value of that concept? VISA, if converted to a stock company, would have an astronomical value. But it cannot be bought, sold, or traded, as ownership is in the form of nontransferable rights of participation.

Value is a concept that Mr. Hock feels strongly about. If money is information, then what is the value of that information?

"We haven't a clue," he posits.

For example, what is intellectual value versus commercial value? What then is natural capital? What are the values that make companies perform? What do we measure in the capital markets, in the financial world, on a balance sheet? Commercial value. Aren't we missing something?

"The balance sheets are all false. They are only a way to aggregate monetary capital," says Mr. Hock. "There is natural capital, intellectual capital, commercial capital, and infrastructure capital," as well as scarcity of capital. None of this is accounted for when we value things—whether they be organizations, commodities or currency, says Mr. Hock. "Our whole system socializes costs and capitalizes gains," he says. "What is it that really concerns the public? Is it the price of the stock market? Nonsense."

He takes a long pause. He knows where all this is headed. Information, you see, has heretofore been bound, locked, kept out of reach. That, as we know, has changed. Access is a mouse click away. That accessibility changes value. It changes most everything—governance, power, and therefore value.

"Information is destroying its boundary asset. Before, there was a difference between public and private information. But all those boundaries have literally dissolved. And evolution isn't going to stop," Mr. Hock says.

There are wild birds overhead. Blue skies. The forests are lush. The air is clean. Water is pure and plentiful. My Imagination sees these things. An Eden.

Then the story gets told. Details are left out. Like a rose petal. Like a bee who gets sent off course in the breeze. You can't account for and capture everything. Reality is too detailed.

Value, without form, is boundless. The limitless information our mind can absorb is the money, the thing we will comprehend in time, Mr. Hock says.

Until then, we are left with data, the storage of the light, the energy that comprises the world.

Only a word can define it. Energy can't be seen. It takes on different representations: the sun, steam heat rising from a sidewalk, electric towers, gas pumps. We see those things and associate energy.

We imagine it, just like money.

Dialogue: Me and My Imagination

"I'm flattered. But aren't we talking about the representation of value? Isn't that what money is?"

"For an imagination, you're rather literal."

"I've got a lot on my mind."

"In fact, you're on to something. Money is what we use to represent value—in its most widely used form. But it doesn't have to be anything. It can just be a word."

"You're putting me to work again, aren't you?"

"Damn straight. I need a picture to move things along. Maybe even a story if you have the time."

"Here goes. But promise me later that you'll watch television, a video, something to replace me so I can rest."

"You got it."

"All right then. You pull up to a nice suburban house. White picket fence, all that. You walk to the front door and knock. A preppy guy holding on to his Great Dane answers. You tell him that he has won a million dollars. The neighbors come out from their houses. A crowd gathers. They are all informed that this guy is now worth a million bucks.

"A house across the street is for sale. The preppy guy says, 'I'll buy that house for $500,000.' His word is all that is transmitted. People believe him because they were just told that he is worth a million dollars. That worth has now been transmitted. The owner of the house takes his word. She can then use that to go purchase other things—or even invest. As long as people believe that she has that worth, she can spend on her word too. And so, on, and so on, as more and more people take the value of her word and store it or pass it on and use it themselves in whatever increments she has determined."

"But words have no boundaries. A person could overspend."

"A ledger with that information would have to be kept."

"Exactly! It's the storage of information, the data, that represents the value. What we use to transact has been erased."

"Can I go to sleep now?"

"Not yet. The ledger is really an exchange, right? That's where one word is exchanged for another, or one thing is exchanged for another. The values are calculated. That value represents money."

"Sounds like Wall Street."

"It is Wall Street."

CHAPTER 7

The Future of Money as a Credit-Based System

Credit, says Nobel Prize–winner Joseph Stiglitz, is the currency of the future. It is what we'll trade with. Indeed, it is what we trade with and on.

Stiglitz's point of view, to some, is deemed rather radical. For some, his views are easy targets of criticism because of the job Stiglitz formerly held: chairman of President Bill Clinton's Council of Economic Advisers.

Whenever you are in or associated with the political realm, criticism is easily launched. Saying that credit will be the currency, or is the currency, we trade on doesn't exactly help matters, either. Because that's where Stiglitz's views get controversial.

"You can be in Malaysia, and someone can determine your creditworthiness instantly," says Stiglitz. "That's what money has become."

The immediacy of information available through advances in technology makes determining creditworthiness easy and accessible—worldwide. So, who needs a dollar to represent that amount of credit? Who, indeed, needs even a credit card like a VISA, or any other form of representative value? Used to be that anonymity forged the necessity of currency, credit cards, checks, or any other form of numeraire—even data.

Now, of course, that has changed.

"You have a credit report," says Stiglitz. "That shows people who you are and what your purchasing power is."

A credit reports indicates your pattern of behavior when it comes to, essentially, trading. How good is your word? The more successful you are, the more money you make, the more purchasing power you obtain. This is all based on behavior and patterns.

Someday—arguably today—your word may in fact be good for it, whatever "it" is. And your word may be all that you need. Your word can be checked and verified, utilizing the information technology at our fingertips today. Your words can then be gauged for trust. Trust and information, the two ingredients of money, available without the necessity of anything tangible. If not today, then most likely the future. And we'll have more on that later. For now, the future of money is shaping up as a graphic representation on your computer screen. Beenz, flooz, cybercash in some form, are facilitating trade over the Internet—

"Hold it. Hold it right there, " My Imagination demands.

"Beenz, flooz?"

"You got it. I can't imagine what those things are? What the hell is a beenz or a flooz?"

"If, pray tell, you'd let me finish, perhaps you'd have a better idea."

"Ideas are about all I have to work with. Do go on."

—to the tune of some $3.5 billion per month, and growing. Expectations are that more than $1 trillion will be spent per year over the Internet in 2010. Even today, half of all Americans make purchases via the Web.

New moneymakers say their service is needed. You can't exactly cram a dollar bill into your computer. Credit card– and bank deposit–backed trading is expensive, and there are still questions about security. So, why not forget adapting currencies designed for this world and design a currency for the cyberworld?

People are trying.

BusinessWeek, in an article on the future of money, says it may soon look like this: "It's payday, and a week's salary has been directly deposited in your bank account. So you log onto your bank's Web site, pay your rent and your credit-card balance, plus the phone and cable-TV bills. You realize your nephew's birthday is coming up, so you e-mail him some Flooz online currency that could be spent at more than seventy online stores. Now your paycheck is spent, and you never even touched a single greenback, nor signed a single check."[2]

That future *BW* wrote about is now.

"In a network society, there will be lots of different electronic currencies," says Robert Levitan, who founded Flooz.

Flooz is a "gift currency." You buy flooz and send it to people over the Internet, sort of like a gift certificate.

"You can move across countries, and it's not a credit card. There is no bank or country loyalty. It transcends all that," says Levitan.

Right, but it still is backed by traditional forms of payment. Even though it's called flooz, the Arabic word for money and French slang for cash, it really isn't.

Beenz, on the other hand, are currency. Beenz are money. Electronic, can-only-spend-'em-on-the-Web, not hard, very hot, cash.

"Enough. I have to interrupt." It's my Imagination again.

"*Pour quoi?*"

"See, even you've fallen into it. I see French teenagers on corners of the Champs Élysées, smoking cigarettes, wearing tight jeans, mocking tourists, counting flooz, asking for flooz. I see an Arabic man in white robe and turban in the desert. His camel is in the background. He buys something from a desert merchant on an oasis. Flooz."

"What about beenz?"

"They're . . . they're . . . well, go on then."

"Consumers can earn beenz for performing 'e-work' online activities, like visiting a Web site, interacting with online business, shopping, or accessing the Internet through a service provider," Beenz, the company, says. "Consumers can spend their beenz at participating Web sites on hundred and thousands of products and services."

"I'm still coming up blank," says my Imagination.

So I had better clarify.

Beenz can be likened to an online frequent flyer award point. Frequent flyer points, membership awards from spending on certain credit cards, and even loyalty points accumulated through long distance telephone use, are cash. They are money. Your action is valued, and you are rewarded with a "thing." That thing has value, which in turn can be used to obtain other things—like upgrades or car rentals. American Express even allows you to redeem award points for merchandise. I can get everything from a set of golf clubs to free investment consulting, merely by trading in the points I received by using my Amex card to purchase goods. I could even trade in points for cash money.

E-cash developers say the cyberworld will eventually make cash money obsolete. What will be the need to exchange something tangible, when computers already track data and inventory? Computers keep ledgers of what is bought and sold. Data are all that is needed to conduct commerce. E-cash is a way to package information, data, and account for its whereabouts.

"I think I get it now. But it takes some work on my end. And I'm imagining that if I'm having problems—being Imagination after all—then most people will have problems with this cybercash."

"You imagine correctly."

Cybercash, in fact, failed. The company that invented the initial online currency went bankrupt—ran out of money, if you will. Interesting if you think about it, sort of like a counterfeiter who goes broke. You'd have to figure he or she wasn't much good. It wasn't that Cybercash wasn't good; it just wasn't being accepted. And that is the dominant factor in the use of money. How widely accepted is whatever it is that is being called money—dollars, yen, rubles.

Green stamps were a popular method of payment in the United States in the 1950s. But green stamps couldn't be taken to another country and traded for anything. They were worthless. Why? The network of acceptance wasn't large enough. People in foreign countries didn't understand what green stamps were. They didn't have enough information, ergo they couldn't trust that a green stamp was valuable.

The Internet is poised to change the way trust and information are transmitted.

Since trust and information, we have established, are the foundations of money, then in today's world that trust and information is available at the speed of sound.

Governments tell us that a dollar is a dollar, a yen is a yen, a peso is a peso. Merchants decide what this will buy. Consumers say what they will pay. Currency traders shout the value of money and determine a currency's worthiness. Stock traders buy and sell millions of dollars of stock on the faith of a verbal agreement. Words, information. Credit, trust. For the currency of the future, this is all that is needed.

"You really don't need hard money. You need something to communicate with. A dollar is just a note, after all. Why can't that note be written in software code and transmitted as data?" asks Charles Cohen, founder of Beenz.

Cybercash, beenz, flooz. There are a lot of names that can be added to the list of e-cash brands. It doesn't matter what the currency of the future is called. It'll be traded on the trust of that brand. The next logical question is which brand will survive, or whether there will be myriad brands. After VISA and Bank Americard, today's Mastercard, were successful, a slew of cards have hit the market, each pitching a unique twist with their brand name. There are bank cards like Discover, Optima, GM, and Ford, which act like VISA and Mastercard, offering preset bank spending limits. There are charge cards like Diner's Club and Amex, which base your credit limit on your spending patterns. There are retail store cards that are only accepted at specific companies or outlets. And there are debit cards, which act like checks, making withdrawals from checking or savings accounts.

Today's smart cards are hybrids of these. They take credit cards and debit cards a step further, because they reduce the need for the card itself.

A smart card has a microprocessor or memory chip embedded in it. This chip stores electronic data, such as bank account information, credit information, and the like. So, when the card is used—let's say, when driving through a toll booth—the microprocessor, or minicomputer, fully equipped with a tiny antenna, signals the toll booth's microprocessor, or reader. The two computers talk and debit your bank account or credit account—however you have the microprocessor programmed—the amount of the toll. This is done as you drive through, no stopping, in a split second.

All that is to say that a smart card is a credit or debit card that can transmit wireless data.

"I'm panting," notes my Imagination.

"Yes, the vision of us driving through a toll booth on Interstate 95 in Connecticut triggered some fond memories. I also see you've got us careening through various drive-thru windows at fast food restaurants. And now, you're trying to put together an image of me at the grocery store checkout stand. Something has to do with my lapel."

"I'm trying to imagine if they can attach a smart card anywhere."

"Let me save you the trouble."

Luxembourg-based Gemplus, the biggest manufacturer of smart cards, says, "The important thing about smart cards is that they are everyday objects that people can carry in their pockets, yet they have the capacity to retain and protect critical information stored in electronic form.

"The smartness of smart cards comes from the integrated circuit embedded in the plastic card. The same electronic function could be performed by embedding similar circuits in other everyday objects, such as key rings, watches, glasses, rings, or earrings. Smart keys are already being used for pay-TV subscriptions.

"The development of contactless card technology was the catalyst for what is known as tags. Tags function like contactless smart cards but are in the form of a ring or even a baggage label. They are generally attached to objects such as gas bottles, cars, or animals and can hold and protect information concerning that object. This allows the object to be managed by an information system without any manual data handling."

"See, I'm being squelched," says my Imagination.

"How so?"

"Whenever I imagine something that comes true, it moves on over to become part of logic. And logic falls under reason's domain."

"But you are still working now. I see that you think you're being very creative and cute by designing a cyborg."

"Well, I had to take all this somewhere."

"Sorry, Charlie."

" . . . no."

"Yes, I'm afraid there's a computer scientist in England who's already embedding himself with microchips."

"If other people did the same. Pretty soon language would become obsolete; the chips would interact with your brain and speak for you. I'm imagining a scene from *Star Trek*."

"Right. You can have a lot of fun with the cyborg thing. But, back to money, Gemplus says already the sound of your voice, the blink of your eye, may be enough."

The company says, "The use of Biometrics will soon mean that a person can be reliably identified by his or her hand, fingerprints, retina of the eye, or sound of the voice. Soon it will be possible to authorize the use of electronic information in smart cards using a spoken word or the touch of a hand.

"Smart cards are a relatively new technology that already affects the everyday lives of millions of people. This is just the beginning and will ultimately influence the way that we shop, see the doctor, use the telephone, and enjoy leisure.

"Modern society needs an enormous amount of information. Computers give us the means to process this information. Smart cards give us a way of individualizing the handling and control of this information.

"The use of smart card technology will benefit the individual and increase the quality of life."

Increasing the quality of life may be an aggrandizement. But the idea of money becoming an indelible part of the human nature—body, mind, and spirit—seems inevitable. This plays into Stiglitz's thesis of credit, because, as you've read over and over, money is trust and information; it's all credit anyway. Technology may enable people to have the facilities to gauge trust because of the nanosecond ability to access information. We may all, in fact, become a part of the Information Superhighway. That said, trust can be gauged without the need for a tangible conduit.

Technology may enable people to unsheathe the hold governments have on trust, as currency itself is being brought closer to the individual, made part of the individual.

Bernard Lietaer, a money scholar who was named the top currency trader in the world, posits that one day, governments themselves may be obsolete as corporations take over the functions of government utilities and services. (Federal Express instead of the United States Postal Service? For-profit schools instead of public ones?) Who, then, will trust fall to? What will happen to money then?

It may, as former Federal Reserve Board chairman Paul Volcker suggests, unify. "I have come to the conviction that the full implication of a truly global system of trade and finance will ultimately be a common currency encompassing most of the world," Volcker says.

This is how, of course, it was at the beginning. Gold knew no nation or state boundaries, nor did silver, or any other commodity used as a signifier of money. One's word was most frequently used, memorialized by a signature or document of trust.

"Can you be trusted?" may be the only barrier to trade in the future. Who are you, as an individual, as a person, to impute that trust?

Dialogue: Me and My Imagination

"Satisfied?"

"About the future? Yes. It's as I suspected. I'm a goner."

"You think?"

"No, I imagine, remember. Thinking is your gig. I imagine that truth will prevail. I will be stilted as will all of the other imaginations out there if the future of money is as you detect."

"Not so. What you are imagining is that the creative process will be hindered by the logic necessitated by computer processing. In this case, microprocessing. In this case, us. If we become the microprocessor, and interact with other microprocessors, only logic will prevail. Imagination, creativity, right brain activity will be reduced. Why put all that nonsense into the program, right?"

"Exactly, there wouldn't be room for, or reason for, me. The concept of 'wouldn't it be nice . . . ' will be completely erased. Why? Because it's superfluous to any situation. It is, or it isn't. That will be the future. Black. White. Ones. Zeros. I'll be put out to pasture with your dreams, hopes, wants, desires. There'll be some giant wasteland of us creative types splashing around somewhere, frolicking, blowing bubbles."

"You may be pushing it some, you know. I remember in Kurt Vonnegut's book *Timequake*,[3] he talks about the demise of, well, you. Not so directly. But it's his point at the end of the book."

Vonnegut writes that we may be able to discover it all, everything in the universe, if we just factor in one new thing: awareness.

Exemplifying, he characterizes, the observation of stars.

"Pick two twinkling points of obsolete light in the sky above us," he asks. " . . . Whatever heavenly bodies those two glints represent, it is certain that the Universe has become so rarefied that for light to go from one to the other would take thousands or millions of years."

But, he goes on, we can see them in a mere second!

"Even if you'd taken an hour . . . something would have passed between where those two heavenly bodies used to be, at, conservatively speaking, a million times the speed of light."

That something, Vonnegut writes, is human awareness.

"That sounds nice."

"He's a good writer. And he said something about nice, too. He said appreciation is the motivator. That's perhaps the endgame. In his words, 'If this isn't nice, what is?' should be the tag line."

"If what isn't nice?"

"There, that's your domain. Whatever you imagine. Whenever you and I come together. When what you imagine gibes with what is real, what is the truth, just what is. There, then, that's what's truly bankable. So, you see, you big ninny, you're not on death row just yet. Appreciation is under your command. And we as humans need that."

"Now you're guessing because I don't always come up with everything you appreciate. I just put it out there, and you catch up. Once in awhile I hit the mark and you appreciate me; other times, well, it's not so pleasant an experience."

"Your ticklers on money, for example."

"Yes. I imagined that new car you bought would make us happy; it didn't. The watch I imagined would make us stand out didn't do the trick. Those fancy clothes I imagined would attract all the girls were useless. I could go on, you know."

"I know. But maybe that's just us. Maybe what we want just isn't going to lead us to happiness, fulfillment, dare I say, self-realization."

"Reality? I'm out of here."

"How do you expect us to go on like this? We have to investigate that—awareness, remember."

"I imagined we would just check out money, what it is, how it evolved, all that. Then we'd talk to a few smart people about what it means. Then maybe we'd finish up with a little discourse from some religious types about what money ought to mean. Nothing too fancy here, just wanted to get a little fuel for what I should be on the look out for as we get closer and closer to asking those big questions you're always on: Who are we? Why are we here? Too much for me, truth be known."

"No one has been able to answer those riddles."

"See? My point exactly. Why bother? Let's stick with money. Why should we go down the path of what makes us who we are when we are on the discourse of money?"

"Must I really spoon feed you everything?"

"I'm just a child at heart, you know."

"Funny you should put it that way."

"Because?"

"Because I think we'll have to go back there, to childhood. It's where we are shaped, formed, and where our values are put upon us."

"And again the tie in with money is . . . "

"Look, if we are going to determine what money means, we have to take what money is—a way for us to get what we want—we have to understand what drives us to what we want, *n'est ce pas?*"

"Enough with the queer French. I get where you are going. But I'm uncomfortable with all this. Shrinks—and I imagine you are going to speak with some shrinks—always try to mess with me: 'The image or imagination we have of a person or situation and the reality of a person or a situation. The truth versus the idea.' God, I hate that."

"Because they chip away at you."

"Of course. They rein me in, keep you on the straight and narrow. That therapy stuff is a killer—mine."

"Yeah, yeah. Stop being so paranoid. We are only going to investigate the nature of the self from the standpoint of psychology. We are not going to get into anything particularly personal."

"You choose your words carefully."

"Well, you never know what's going to come up."

"So, let me get this straight. We are going to get into the determinants of what makes us our self?"

"Exact-a-mundo."

"I'm asking because I imagine this ties back into the last line of the last chapter: 'Who are you, as an individual, as a person, to impute that trust?'"

"Right. We apply what money is to the self."

"Humanize it."

"*Oui.*"

"Enough!"

The Psychological Attachment of Money: What Money Means

CHAPTER 8

Toward Self-Realization

To humanize the constructs of money, I have turned to a theorem by an old fellow who has been both hailed and chastised. Proven right. Proven wrong. Some still agree with his thesis (like me), and some don't (ask around).

The person whom I'm speaking of is Abraham Maslow, the psychologist who designed our (read: human) hierarchy of needs. The thesis is rather simple: We fulfill our basic needs on a bottom-up basis. We need food first, then shelter, then a sense of belonging, a degree of esteem. After all those needs are met, we can aim for self-actualization. Self-actualization, or self-realization, is "[the] moments of greatest maturity, individuation, fulfillment," writes Maslow in *Toward A Psychology of Being.*[4]

Maslow's critics say you don't need to be hungry before you need to be successful. I disagree. The more evolved our needs become, the more we try to satiate those desires. And you *do* need to be hungry before you can evolve toward a more sophisticated palate.

The idea that money can lead us down this path of satiation is even more compelling, because money is the promulgator; it's what allows needs to be filled most rapidly. Hungry? Buy a burger. Cold? Shut the door and turn on the heat. Want to belong? Join a country club.

The basic needs that Maslow promotes are easily attainable through monetary measures. But this only goes about halfway up what some call the "pyramid" that Maslow defined. Love and belonging are right smack in the middle of Maslow's hierarchy, and it's here where money begins to sputter. Myriad motivations kick in for self-fulfillment. Someone may write to get published—for the recognition, rather than for the money. Writing, for the money-grubber, may not lead to self-fulfillment of the ego, or any other emotional quality. Instead, writing may be a curse if, say, dancing is the true desire.

"I'm imagining you—"

"Don't even go there."

Carl Rogers, another psychologist and a contemporary of Maslow, put forth a theory that we all have the drive to develop to our fullest potential. He said that human beings have an "actualizing" tendency that works through everything. Some of us don't reach that goal, which interferes with our accomplishments, sense of self and ego, and, ultimately, our self-realization or actualization.

Here, the real self gets split from the ideal self. In Maslow's theory, love and belonging separate the two.

"I imagine you are speaking of the difference between me and you now?" asks my Imagination.

"I was leaving that to the reader."

"Sorry to wreck such subtlety, but if you are going to say that the difference between me and you is love and belonging, then I think you have more problems than even I imagined."

"Why is that?"

"Because if I am based on expectations, then those expectations had to come from somewhere. If they came from somewhere else, they aren't yours or mine. I can only imagine the things that separate us are the things that have influenced us both."

"Sigmund Freud believed that we are influenced by our childhood obsessions, our needs from that time. Those influences shape us, he said, they provide the expectations and, dare I say it, form you. But your point is well taken."

If the ideal self can be separated from the self, then the question becomes, Can it ever be put back again? Fulfillment is completeness, feeling whole. We can't be whole if one side of us is imagining that life would be better another way. We can't be whole if one side of us imagines that there is something more. That puts the real self in jeopardy. The real self becomes pained and suffers, knowing that life could indeed be better somewhere else, somehow.

Victor Frankl, a student of Freud's, tried to make sense out of all this. He said that in order to find meaning in life, we have to understand our pain, or what makes us unhappy. The rationale: to become happy you must understand unhappiness.

Once the understanding of pain and suffering prevails, we understand what's important to our lives. Once we understand what's important, we can pursue those things. And once we are empowered with those values, we can assign meaning to our lives. That's the endgame, the pursuit of meaning.

As I further examine the humanistic approach to psychology, it becomes readily apparent that something is missing: the human.

Sure, all the theories are nice and well put. They define pain. They define suffering. They even give the solutions to ending pain and suffering. But all this is based on empirical data, facts derived from test groups and certain kinds of people. Who are these people?

The people I'm interested in are the ones who can help me and my Imagination figure out if our expectations of money are true.

What could we expect if we had a million dollars? What would life be like? What would it mean?

What could we expect if we, well, couldn't even imagine a million dollars? What would it mean, how would we be?

My Imagination, of course, is the one being tested. We have uncovered what money really is. We have defined the constructs of money, talked to the scholars, read the books, and now understand the defining principles of money and what money may become.

Defining what money means is an awfully personal endeavor. What money means to me is different than what money means to every other person on this planet. Or is it? Are there some commonalities that we can explore and investigate to get to the bottom of the situational meaning of money?

Today, the world is the most prosperous it has ever been. Despite any economic slips, the average family today has more money to spend. Period. Fact. And the cultural focus, in the United States anyway, is more and more about money. Entire television networks are dedicated to following money's path on a minute-by-minute basis. Talking heads on the floor of the New York Stock Exchange blab about the value of this and the value of that. Analysts uncover new value. They dispute existing value. They change the way people feel about their money, about themselves.

"Money makes people feel richer," Maria Bartiromo tells me. Maria is fondly known as "The Money Honey." She is a television news anchor for the all-business, all-the-time news station CNBC and the first woman to report from the floor of the New York Stock Exchange. "People are better equipped with information. They are more money-savvy."

What Maria is really saying is that people are more empowered by money and knowledge. The stock market is a different story. "People think an investment in the stock market is money; it's not. It's paperless. It's an illusion," Maria says.

Even though it's not cash in hand, highs and lows in the stock market change how people feel. The feeling of empowerment. The feeling of success, winning. "It's the wealth effect," Maria tells me.

She's about to talk. The stock market has gyrated back and forth, up and down, every which way it can. Ebullient investors counting their stock market winnings are concerned. Some are upset. Many are suffering losses.

Money's tie to feeling good or feeling bad has to do with how much or how little of it you have. But is that really the case? Are we setting ourselves up for a gigantic fall if we expect that the more money we have, the better we will feel?

The following chapters sketch a portrait of feelings and expectations discerned by the concept of money. Drawn from Maslow's hierarchy of needs, my Imagination and I will explore what today's leading psychologists have to say about money. Then we will satisfy the human element, garnering interpretations from some of the poorest people in the world as well as from some of the richest, with some comments from those in between. Through it all money will play the central role. It will become a feeling. Like any other feeling, it is subject, and apt, to change, to be misunderstood, to be yearned for, to be overwhelming, to be ignored, and to be relished.

Money, like the thoughts rummaging around in our heads, needs to be defined by experience. Hopefully, we can find those experiences that will shed the most light and catch meaning by surprise.

CHAPTER 9

The Disconnect of Money from Quality of Life

I'm waiting to see my shrink, Dr. Joel Bergman. I'm in the cluttered waiting room just outside Joel's office. He makes you sit on deck chairs, stare at a broken, old coffee maker, scan books on marriage counseling, listen to the city traffic through an open window, wonder about the video monitor that is hooked to a camera in his office. Joel never sees you right away. There are these tormented minutes. I think it's part of strategy to give you time to reflect on why you're there.

I can never stand to sit and stare and wonder. I pick up the books, read, rummage through what I can. Some days I'll even take out a magazine of my own and get through an article before I "hit the couch."

Today—it's not, but let's call it today—I peruse the clippings, Post-Its, and comics that Joel has tacked and taped to the front door (just below the cow bell). A photocopy of an article that ran in the op-ed section of the *New York Times* catches my eye. I read. It catches my attention. I read on. It fully intrigues me, so much so that I rip it off the door and ask Joel to photocopy it again for me.

The article is called "The Pursuit of Affluence, At a High Price."[5] It talks about psychological research that shows money doesn't indeed buy happiness. "Not only does having more things prove to be unfulfilling, but people for whom affluence is a priority in life tend to experience an unusual degree of anxiety and depression as well as a lower overall level of well-being," the article, written by Alfie Kohn, says. He says two psychologists have done groundbreaking work in the area of self-determination, studying different groups of people around the world and in different income brackets. Seems it doesn't matter where you live or how much money you have or make. The same conclusion is made through all the studies that these psychologists have conducted: The more we seek satisfaction in material goods, the less satisfied we become.

I'm excited. I tell Joel of what a find this is. How much these guys can help me, if they will, with my book.

Joel doesn't know what the hell I'm talking about. He'd forgotten what the article said. "I put that up for my yuppie clients," Joel says.

But first let me back up a step. I have to explain Joel.

Dr. Joel Bergman is a well-known psychologist, a practitioner who has taught and lectured around the world. His specialty: pain and suffering, that which stems from relationships. He focuses on marriage counseling. It's his specialty that got us together. I was going through a divorce, and turned to Joel for help. He helped me, in that New York way: Identify the pain and deal with it.

Joel is a native New Yorker. His office is in the Village. He says, "You're acting crazy." (An upsetting sentence coming from your shrink.) He doesn't say, "Tell me"; he tells me. When my ex-wife did something particularly painful, which I couched and forgave, he says, "Fuck her. What are you, a pussy?"

So when I speak with Joel about the meaning of money, which we got on to immediately after he copied the *New York Times* article for me, I expected another "What-the-fuck-are-you-talking-about?" response. It wasn't like that. Rather, Joel, who prefers old leather chairs to couches in his office, who keeps Hershey kisses in a jar, who is a bit slouched, who has thick skin and thinning gray hair, who looks like a bird and dresses in drab shirts and slacks like a liberal arts college professor, doesn't answer me right away. He is quiet. "Let me think about that," Joel says.

I know Joel. When Joel thinks about something, he really *thinks* about it— and he ain't stupid. Joel catches me on my oft-pretentious recitations of Goethe, of Dante, of Wittgenstein and Freud. "What are you, some type of throwback?" he says. "We live here . . . now." He points to the floor. "You're the King of the Nile." But he pronounces the "the" as a "d" so it comes out "denial." Then he catches himself and laughs. Joel always laughs at his own witticisms, even if they're not that funny.

So I decide to ask Joel about what money means to him. More silence ensues. I figure at my next session he'll have an answer, some type of response. We move on in our discussion to other matters.

It's a day later—okay, it isn't a day later, but let's call it a day later—and Joel sends me an e-mail. It's an analogy. It's only a couple of paragraphs long, but it answers my question about what money means to him in full. It gives me insight, makes me think. And I remember why Joel is so good at what he does:

He's sneaky. In his sneaky way, he teaches me about myself. I imagine he does the same for others too. He catches me off guard with the e-mail. And he further surprises me with the depth and simplicity of his response.

Joel writes me this story of a fisherman in a Mexican village who goes out every day on his boat to catch fish. The fisherman goes out for three or four hours, catching a small load of fish and returning home. Every day he does this, without fail. One week, an investment banker from New York is vacationing in this Mexican village. Every day he sees this young fisherman go out, catch fish, come back, go out, catch fish, come back. So, after a few days, the investment banker approaches the fisherman. He asks the fisherman if he catches fish like that all the time.

"I do," says the young Mexican, who is about thirty years old.

"How long have you been fishing?" asks the investment banker.

"All my life," says the Mexican. "Since I was a boy."

"And you catch fish like that every time?" He looks at the sizable fish in the catch.

"Yes," says the Mexican. "There are always fish."

"But you only go out a few hours a day. If you catch fish like that, why don't you go out longer—catch more fish?"

The young Mexican thinks a minute and looks down at his feet. He looks back up at the investment banker. "Well, I like to spend time with my family and play cards with my friends."

The investment banker nods, he steps closer to the Mexican. "Look," he says, "if you double the amount of time you fish, you'll make double the amount of money you make now."

"Why would I want to do that?" asks the Mexican.

"Because then you can buy another boat and hire more fishermen."

"Why would I want to do that?" asks the Mexican again.

"Because then you'll quadruple your earnings and pretty soon you can have your own fleet."

"And why would I want to do that?"

"Well, once you have your own fleet, you'll have enough fish to cut out the middle men and go directly to the distributor. You do well enough with him, you can buy his company. Then, we do an IPO, take the whole operation public. You'll cash in. You'll be rich."

"And then what?"

"Then," says the investment banker, "you can spend time with your family, and play cards with your friends . . . "

I read over Joel's e-mail several times. It's in a tiny box on the corner of my computer screen. My Imagination pictures the Mexican village, on a small bay dotted with boats. He sees the red Spanish tile roofs of the homes that wind along the tiny roads. He sees a shirtless young, bronzed Mexican fisherman wearing pale, yellowed linen pants, espadrilles, and a straw hat. He sees this young man standing on a dock, speaking with a man almost twice his age. The older man—this investment banker—is dressed in Docker shorts, Nike sneakers, and a polo shirt. The man is wearing large, black sunglasses. The Mexican is squinting. My Imagination pictures their body language. The investment banker: chest forward, shoulders high, his chin creeping more and more past his toes as his neck stretches, emphasizing his speech. The young Mexican: resting back on his heels, arms folded over his chest, his sternum pulling farther and farther away from the investment banker.

My Imagination wonders whether the investment banker gets it, whether he understands how ridiculously circular his plan is—his life is. He sees the frustration in the investment banker. He figures the investment banker chalks up the lack of enthusiasm to laziness, to stupidity. My Imagination has the banker storming away, maybe lighting a cigar halfway around the U-shaped bay. He sees the Mexican just staring at the banker as he lights the cigar and, perhaps, even talks on a mobile phone. My Imagination sees a young Mexican boy run over to the fisherman and take his hand. The fisherman and the boy head in the opposite direction of the banker, who is now walking toward the other end of the U. The boy and the fisherman don't look over at the banker, and he doesn't look back at them. They seem to have forgotten about each other, as if their conversation never existed. They just couldn't understand what money meant to the other.

Dialogue: Me and My Imagination

"We seem to have taken a turn."

"Be brief, I want to move on with things."

"It's more about you now, isn't it?"

"What do you mean?"

"I'm more empowered by this knowledge, these stories, these experiences. It's you who's being diminished."

"In what way?"

"The more you experience what I imagine, the less hope there seems to be for any other life than the one you are leading."

"Yes, escapism doesn't seem to work so well."

"I can keep imagining new places, new things, new wants, hopes, dreams, desires. But if you know them to be false, I'll have wasted my time and effort. You'll get depressed."

"The pursuit of affluence, you're saying, will squelch me more than you."

"From what little you've read, I imagine that to be the case.

"Let's see."

CHAPTER 10

The Empirical Study of Hedonic and Eudaimonic Well-Being

Imagination aside, it's this lack of understanding between wealth-seekers and peace-seekers that has me on the hunt for Dr. Richard Ryan and Dr. Tim Kasser. They are the two psychologists who look at "the dark side of the American dream." They say that chasing money makes people mentally ill. They say materialism breeds depression, not happiness—and they have case studies to prove it.

I track down Ryan at the University of Rochester in New York, and he agrees to an interview. This and the research papers, articles, and other discussions about "self determination" theory give me a pretty good idea of what Ryan and Kasser have discovered about the pursuit of affluence. And while it's difficult to say that it's dark, it is, at least, a gray area.

"When we started out, we were looking at people's value systems and their emphasis on relationships, commitment, and personal growth," says Ryan. "When we put the relative importance value on money, it had strong mental effects."

Unhappiness.

Indeed, it wasn't the intent of the studies to show that the pursuit of affluence created unhappiness, it just turned out that way, according to Dr. Richard Ryan, professor in the Department of Clinical and Social Sciences in Psychology at the University of Rochester.

I drop the "doctor" after a few moments with Ryan. He is a casual, more accessible fellow than such a title affixes. He speaks informally, as well; no esoteric psychology jargon was put to me.

Things are "happy," or "sad."

That was surprising, considering some of the titles of Ryan's work: "A Meta-Analytic Review of Experiments Examining the Effects of Extrinsic Rewards on Intrinsic Motivation,"[6] "On Happiness and Human Potentials: A Review of Research on Hedonic and Eudaimonic Well-Being,"[7] and so on.

Ryan steered our interview away from esoteric methodology toward real-life, touchy-feely questions and answers.

"We all think there is satisfaction in shopping, right? But when people make purchases, there is actually an upswing in negative effect," says Ryan. "When my wife comes up and gives me a hug, there is nothing dissatisfying in that."

Simple pleasures mean the most.

Ryan's work, and thesis, basically say that most people are barking up the wrong tree. "People who had financial success also had discontent with their family relationships and their caring relationships. If I wake up and all I think about is the next consulting job or the next seminar and my kid is asking me a question about something important to him but I'm too preoccupied to pay attention, there is a problem—for the child and for me."

Money, says Ryan, doesn't help, nor does it seem to hurt personal well-being.

"Because it's about being rich. The other part is fine. When your personal well-being is attached to the attainment of goals, and the attainment of those goals doesn't produce happiness, look out," says Ryan.

. . . And then, depression sets in.

"Our intrinsic values have to be satisfying in their own right," says Ryan. "If they happen to have an extrinsic benefit, that's happenstance."

Play the game because you love it.

"After the 1960s and now, after two periods of affluence, people are asking 'What now?' more and more. When we get things, we realize that we aren't all that satisfied by them," says Ryan.

Philanthropy is up more than 1,000 percent over the last five years.

The material, or extrinsic, things that Ryan speaks of can never replace the internal, or intrinsic, needs that Ryan speaks of. Try as we might.

Rosebud.

In his findings, Ryan studied a group of eighteen-year-olds, about three hundred of them from Russia and the United States. Among most of the individuals who wanted material trappings, the majority had mothers who were cold or distant to them as children.

"They want material trappings because they have promises of what comes with them, which is intimacy and a sense of security and love. It doesn't happen. If someone loves you because of your car, it means that they don't love you. So you can't win," Ryan says.

I drive a Porsche and date a model.

This happens with couples too. "When you are with someone because they look good, and their looks somehow, you think, will reflect upon you, that's not a start to a healthy relationship. You have to find a spiritual partner, someone you can relate to on a deeper level," says Ryan.

The soul.

How do we get there? How do we escape from these "surface trappings," as Ryan calls them, and go deep?

"Those people who are higher in mindfulness and are attuned to what's going on around them are also attuned to their intrinsic values."

Consciousness.

"Those who contribute, who are caring toward others and for the earth, can find intrinsic satisfaction even though happiness wasn't the goal."

The formal thesis:

> Self-determination theory (SDT) is another perspective that has both embraced the concept of eudaimonia, or self-realization, as a central definitional aspect of well-being and attempted to specify both what it means to actualize the self and how that can be accomplished. Specifically, SDT posits three basic psychological needs—autonomy, competence, and relatedness—and theorizes that fulfillment of these needs is essential for psychological growth (e.g. intrinsic motivation), integrity (e.g. internalization and assimilation of cultural practices), and well-being (e.g. life satisfaction and psychological health), as well as the experiences of vitality and self-congruence. Need fulfillment is thus viewed as a natural aim of human life that delineates many of the meanings and purposes underlying human actions.

My Imagination wants a word or two: A long, stretch of a road cutting through the desert. Heat blurs the road about a foot above the tar. The yellow line, broken by dashes, skidmarks, and weather, looks as if it dips and rises in curves leading to a large slice between the towering, jagged red rock hills ahead. The sky is white, patched with blue. Nothing is in sight. Nothing appears. Nothing is there to indicate that anything will, in fact, move—ever. Just the sand. Maybe a scrappy plant's dead leaf. Nothing much will move, that is unless I stroll by and stir things up. But I don't notice my surroundings. I walk on.

How to satisfy a sense of love and belonging? How to satisfy a sense of competence and autonomy? These values and the fulfillment of them begin at mindfulness. "Usually it begins with mindfulness: how attuned are you to people and what's going on around you," says Ryan.

Once that consciousness approaches, the path to fulfillment is an individual journey. That can take many routes. But the road to riches doesn't seem to be the one to take.

Dialogue: Me and My Imagination

"You're killing me here."

"Why? You had your little bit about the desert."

"Not that. If all those things I equate with having money—mansions, jets, cars, pretty girls—are bollix, and you, armed with this new information you've gotten, begin to presuppose that they, in fact, are, I'll get gypped out of even more things I associate with happiness."

"More things?"

"Yes. I imagined all sorts of things were gonna make us happy. There was that Big Wheel."

"I rode it down the stairs, flipped onto the sidewalk, and sprained a wrist."

"The mini-bike."

"The throttle stuck and I tumbled over some shrubs."

"Skis."

"Broke my nose."

"Silk shirts."

"I attracted guys, not girls."

"Earring."

"Ditto."

"Marriage."

'That's different."

"It wasn't what I imagined."

"Okay, okay. I get your point. But there still is room for you to produce happiness. You're just focused on the wrong things."

"I got news for you, bubba, I only work with what I have. These inputs are what make me: memories and present happenings. That's all I got. Your experiences, contacts, and associations in this world."

"Those are shaped by family, friends, society, and culture."

"I can imagine that at some point, however, I won't need any of them anymore."

"Perhaps. But I'm not sure about that. Before we decide where and when money becomes an apparent force in the world, we have to investigate what we base that force upon. And how that fits into our hierarchy of needs."

"I can tell you for sure that I wasn't imagining squat about money before the age of five."

"When . . . "

"When your first tooth fell out and we woke up with a dollar bill under our pillow. I started to imagine what we could do with that money."
"It became a concept. From there, all sorts of things began to happen. We could participate in society."
"And I didn't imagine it would all turn out like this, that we would have to think of ways to earn more. I just imagined we'd continue to get it—somehow. I never did put much thought into how until later."
"By then it was too late. We had already become a consumer."

CHAPTER 11

The Childhood Development of Value

People, posits psychoanalyst Theodore Kurtz, are focused on the wrong things to make themselves happy.

"We have built a society around the concept of consume, consume, consume. It's commercialism. It's advertising. It's what we are told will make us happy. Buy things. But that is exactly the opposite of the case," he says.

Kurtz is a Freudian. He follows the thesis that our childhood shapes much of our personality. It's during that period that our psychological pain and happiness live. To alleviate the pain, to uncover the happiness, we must confront our childhood memories.

Kurtz isn't your every day psychoanalyst either. He specializes in financial issues. He writes a column for financial advisers in a trade magazine called *Registered Representative*. He focuses his skills on helping individuals cope with money issues and advisers cope with people who have to confront money issues. He lives and works on Long Island's North Shore, where old money resides and where new money encroaches.

It's a telling geographical intersection—people who've had lots of money for lots of generations and people who've just made lots of money for the first time. Both can learn lessons of appreciation from the other.

"'How much is enough?' is an issue I deal with all the time," says Kurtz. "The problem is there is usually no amount of money that feels right. It keeps going up."

Kurtz says that Freud examined the issue of money and happiness.

"He examined whether money could provide happiness. And what he came up with was that happiness would be the fulfillment of early childhood wishes. Money was never a childhood wish," Kurtz says. Ergo, no amount of money can buy happiness.

That could have been the end of the discussion between Kurtz and me. But I decide to try and delve deeper into the matter.

My Imagination sees a man holding a check. The man is seated in an office. The door is closed. The man, in his fifties, is wearing a shirt and tie. A blue blazer is hung on a hanger on the back of his office door. There are a few books arranged on shelves across from where he is seated. There are some pictures on the wall. Some awards, some memorabilia. On his desk is a bronze statuette of a baseball. On its base a small plaque reads I PLAY HARDBALL.

The man takes off his glasses and continues to stare at the check. It reads $3 million. It's dated February 1, 2001. The man smiles. He leans back in his chair.

"The pursuit of money becomes an addiction. If you cross the finish line, you no longer have the pursuit. And it's the chase that gets them high," Kurtz says.

Another check is being held by the same man that my Imagination pictured before. The man is seated in the same office, in the same position. This time, the check reads $3 million, too, but it's dated February 1, 2002. The man angrily slams the check down on his desk and shakes his head. He stands up and leaves, storming out of the office.

The same as last year isn't more this year. In this man's mind, he failed to beat his own expectations.

Kurtz says, "What many people attach to money is a statement about themselves. They think people judge them by it. For women, their pocketbook is the opening sign in terms of status, or their shoes. This is acceptance. It's a code to indicate 'You're okay.'"

The "you're okay" part Kurtz is discussing falls into Maslow's hierarchy in the categorical need for love and belonging. Country clubs, he points out, are indicators of this need. "A group is defined," says Kurtz. "Who is accepted and who isn't. It's us versus them. And the 'us' gives a sense of security."

Safety and security are also important psychological issues that many people try to mask through such things as gated communities. They believe that safety can be obtained by adding more and more locks. This will make them feel more and more safe, Kurtz says. "But the thing is, this only increases the anxiety," he says.

It's the same with money, according to Kurtz. "You can't get safety through money. And you can't get security through a mentality of 'us' and 'them.'"

Why?

"This undermines closeness and contact. You continue to feel more and more isolated. More and more gates are put up. And you have to worry more about the money that you need to validate who you are," Kurtz says.

My Imagination sees a bearded Howard Hughes driving an old, red pickup truck down a desert highway.

Kurtz and I discuss the paranoia money can promulgate. We discuss how the "more" factor becomes like dogs chasing a rabbit on a track. "And once the dogs realize it's fake, they cease to chase the rabbit," says Kurtz.

Realization: that's the tough part. Some dogs die without ever realizing the rabbit was fake. Some dogs retire early; they stop running.

People get around to realization in different ways. I mention to Kurtz that a number of the rich people that I'd interviewed on the subject of money and fulfillment had suffered some type of loss. They either had been sick, or some other tragedy had occurred to arouse a sense of consciousness about money and its power. Money, it seemed, in large amounts bred dispiritedness and even illness.

"The problem with money is that it's used to seed a side of consumerism as opposed to production," says Kurtz. "When consumerism doesn't make you happy, your whole value system becomes false. You fall into a funk. You can get depressed. Sure, you can become ill.

"Money for consumerism is tantamount to junk food—there's not a lot of nourishment, so you need to keep consuming. You have to balance consumption with productivity. It's that nutrition that provides the real growth."

In other words, do something—don't just buy something. How much more of a sense of accomplishment is derived from doing something yourself than buying something from someone else?

"When I work with children of wealthy parents, the first thing I have them do is produce something—whether it's playing an instrument or making something with their hands. It creates goals," says Kurtz.

The goals for money come in two parts.

"Money is a commodity and a useful commodity. It can be used to buy things. And then once you have enough of that commodity, then you can use money for freedom," says Kurtz.

That is the normal thinking. That is the goal. But that is false.

"Money doesn't create freedom. It's a prison, because it controls you," says Kurtz. "The one commodity you can't get back in life is time."

He says the focus of life should be on how we spend our time. In the most productive manner. In the most meaningful way.

"Am I doing what I want to do with the time I have?" should be the question, says Kurtz. "That activates the decisions and the values that make us happy."

But there are forces against us.

"As far as we've gone as a society, we haven't gone very far with money. At all levels of our culture, it's misused. The wrong values are reinforced. The government reinforces this. The tax code reinforces this. Ultimately, we as a people have to decide what we want to encourage or discourage. And as far as messages, they are all toward consumerism. Advertising is geared toward consumers, not producers," says Kurtz.

Of course this is the case. We are inundated with calls, commercials, provocation to buy, buy, buy. What, at the end of the day, are we buying, however?

"It's all a sense of belonging and being hip," says Kurtz. This, he says, goes back in society to idolatry. You worship something because of what it seems to provide. "You want the idol to give you something," says Kurtz. "If you worship the idol, you make a contract. If you worship, this is what you'll get in return. And, most often, that was safety."

Today, it's much the same. "You'll be wanted, desirable, looked upon," says Kurtz. Inherent in this, however, is existential anxiety. "We are a culture of people who belong. In the Amish culture, punishment is to be shunned. In jail, solitary confinement is the worst punishment," says Kurtz.

We do what we have to do not be alone.

"Money insulates us from aloneness," says Kurtz.

The ultimate aloneness is death. This is the fear we are constantly fighting, whether we acknowledge it or not.

There are those that choose not to acknowledge this. They shun money. They make the "anti" statement. "They say, 'We are not going to be like you,'" says Kurtz. "What they are trying to prevent is the problem. In shunning money, they are also being controlled by it. It's just the other side of the same coin."

Control is the goal. People who overspend are trying to recapture their youth. They are reverting to their childhood. They don't want to grow up. Growing up is getting old, it's closer to death. It's closer to being alone. If you always use up your money, you can never get ahead. And never getting ahead means that you aren't conforming. It, too, is a rebellion.

Money is looking for a need of gratification. In what way am I trying to fulfill that need? If I can get a handle on that need, I can control it, and not have it control me.

Money, says Kurtz, needs to be controlled. Otherwise, people are consumed by it.

My Imagination sees the man in the office with the $3 million check. He puts down the check, now dated 2003. He runs his hands through his hair. He leans back in his chair and looks at a calendar, which sits upright facing him. The date is circled: February 1. It says FATHER-SON BASKETBALL GAME. The man looks at his watch. He curses. He stands, taking his wallet from his back pocket. He takes the check from his desk and when he opens his wallet to place the check in it, a dollar bill leaps out and gobbles him whole.

The $3 million check floats, like any other piece of paper, to the ground. The man's chair swings round and round. The wallet is on the floor, leafed open. Next to it, a single dollar bill lies by itself.

Dialogue: Me and My Imagination

"Death, that's happy."

"It's what you and I are fighting against most of the time."

"I try not to imagine what it would be like to be dead."

"I don't suppose you could even imagine it if you tried. Hence, our devotion to certain religion and faiths."

"They do my job for me."

"And when it comes to money and what it means, death certainly puts it in perspective."

"That's why I'm so useful when you think about money; it's for the here and now."

"You certainly can't take it with you."

"You could die trying, I imagine."

"Lots of people have. There's that story of the sinking ship and the man who tied a bag of gold around his waist so he wouldn't die broke. There's the story of Midas, of course, whose every touch turned things to gold, but who forgot to exclude food, water, and people, ostracizing him from society. Money, enough of it anyway, may be the next closest thing to immortality, but it comes with its consequences."

"I imagine the pursuit is really for all that power—knowing that you could buy everything and anything. See, what fun."

"Of course that's the illusion. It's false. Money can't buy time—as Kurtz just explained."

"But it can certainly make the time we have a little more fun—allows me to get creative anyway."

"Until, of course . . . "

"Don't say 'the end.' I can't imagine an end. In my world, everything goes on and on. Even after we die, I imagine a continuum."

"That's why, I suppose, it's so important to understand what money means in the here and now."

"I thought that was part of the concept of self-realization we were getting to."

"It is. But it seems to me that before we move up the Maslowian pyramid, we have to define some of these constructs so you'll have someplace to go in case things don't work out."

"You mean if I die?"

"I mean if your use is no longer needed in the context of putting me to use—in applying creativity to a futile notion."

"Death. Futility. Pain. Suffering. This doesn't sound like happy talk, or my type of place. I'm usually best at imagining things can get better. Of course once in awhile I get into a funk and all I can imagine is bad stuff."

"Trust me, I know. I suffer the consequences."

"So how do you propose we resolve this conflict for good?"

"The usual, talk with somebody who's explored these things before."

CHAPTER 12

Suffering and Money

On my search for money's place in the world, how it attaches to pain, suffering, emotional displacement, I speak with lots of people. I interview lots of people. I inquire about attitudes, sentiments, and general beliefs in what money means, whether it's a positive or negative force in life, and how this all weaves together to create this wondrous fabric of humanity.

Along the way, I meet people who know people whom I've met before. I meet people who've met people who know people who know me, and so on. The world, in that rationale of six degrees of separation, sometimes feels quite small.

George Kinder is one of those people who, through other people, has landed on my interview list. I find out at once that there is more than one George Kinder, however. There is George Kinder the financial adviser. There is George Kinder the poet. There is George Kinder the Buddhist teacher. There's even a George Kinder who works in Massachusetts and one who works in Maui, Hawaii. Guess what? They're all the same George Kinder.

He's an intriguing one, this George.

George is part of a new vein of financial adviser who bridges the gap between psychology and finance. They call themselves different things— behaviorists, advisers, planners, analysts—but the central thesis behind this group of counselors is that there is more to money than investing

There is a psychological attachment to money that most financial planners leave behind with a savings plan on the kitchen table. There is a goal, not a number, that people want to achieve. There is a reason for this goal in their lives. When these new financial advisers hear from their clients, "I want to retire at age sixty-five," they strive to understand why a person wants to retire at age sixty-five, how they see their lives, and what they imagine their lives to be like.

George Kinder has fashioned a lecture series and workshop on this type of goal-setting. From it, a book spawned: *The Seven Stages of Money Maturity*. [8]

George, in all of this, explores what money means. "You should really speak with him," was what I was told. So, I do.

I call George on the telephone and schedule an interview with him. Meanwhile, he suggests that I read his book. All authors suggest you read their books.

In George's book, he talks about innocence, pain, knowledge, understanding, vigor, vision, and aloha. These are the seven stages to resolving those inner conflicts around money, as he calls it. It's about becoming at ease with money, realizing that money isn't how much, but "What does it have to do with who I am?"

George's seven stages portend to get people to that point of discovery.

As a Buddhist, of course, George infuses some of his spiritual lingo into his financial philosophy. He'll talk about *chakras*—those sections of the body that represent certain emotions, like pain, suffering, love, and fear. He'll talk about *samsara*, and the cycle of life. He'll cite passages from the *Bodhicaryavatara*, a Tibetan Buddhist poem. As a Buddhist, he comes from a perspective that we're all suffering. The essential question is how to stop the pain.

George devised his seven stages to help people stop the pain associated with money.

Stage one: Innocence. This represents the beliefs, thoughts, stories, attitudes, and assumptions about money that we hold on to. Stage two: Pain. This has to do with the conflict, guilt and, shame that surround money. Stage three: Knowledge. This is the practical side of money, such as saving, investing, financial planning. Step four: Understanding. This is patience and realizing that things don't always work out at first as we wish. Stage five: Vigor. This is the enthusiasm to find what constitutes freedom in the world of money. Stage six: Vision. This is focus and directs our sense of life purpose. Stage seven: Aloha. This is connecting with the world, wholly, deeply, and truthfully.

The seven stages speak for themselves. They are a process by which one can embark toward self-discovery. But I'm more interested in having George tell me what money means to him.

So, I show up at George's office in Harvard Square, I climb the two flights of stairs required to reach his office, and I ask him the question: What does money really mean—to him? A simple answer I don't get. And, given how I've described George's various interests and manifestations, that shouldn't come as any big surprise.

First, he tells me about Nasrudin.

Nasrudin was a mullah, the equivalent of a prophet, who lived sometime between the eighth and eleventh centuries A.D.

"People not only don't know when he lived, but they don't know where he lived," George says. "He is claimed by Morocco, by Lebanon, by Egypt, by Turkey—I think there are eight different countries that claim him. But he was a Sufist. And in the Sufi tradition there are always these stories, and Nasrudin stories are the kind you'd see on the bottom of Bazooka bubble gum—the little jokes. So, the one that I always introduce is the one where he goes into what is the equivalent of a bank in the Middle Ages, and he asks 'Can I transact some business?' And the teller says 'Well, sure you can, but can you identify yourself first?' And he says, 'Well, yeah.' So he reaches into his satchel and he takes out a mirror and he gazes into it and he turns back to her and says, 'Yeah, that's me all right.'"

George laughs heartily at the story, his joke, as if he has told it for the first time. In fact, I find out he has told this same story in hundreds of speeches to individuals, associations, and other financial planners. It's George's way of setting you up. He then gets serious.

George is seated at a large, round table in his office. I can hear the traffic noise from below. As he changes gears, the energy shifts. His body movements still. He looks at me more directly. I hear the sound of traffic. And then I don't—George fills the void.

"Nasrudin's stories are filled with money. Lots of money stories. But they also have this undercurrent, not only as humor, as paradox, but a deeper meaning. The Sufis are always looking for a deeper meaning. And the deeper meaning ascribed to that particular story is that money is about us. It's not about a set of numbers or net worth, it's about who we are. So, Nasrudin was sort of puncturing that myth, that balloon."

The balloon punctures and gold coins fall out. They spread onto the hardwood floors of George's office. They spread out into the anteroom, where his assistant sits. The level of the coins gets higher and higher, filling the room, covering us. I think that we are going to drown in coins, suffocate, get buried. As the coins surround my neck and shoulders and creep up past my chin, I start to panic. The rest of my body is immobile. The heavy coins have me trapped and paralyzed from the neck down. As the first coin reaches my nostrils, I take a deep breath in and relax. I close my eyes. When I open them, George is there, just as before. He hasn't missed a beat. Neither has my recorder, as my Imagination runs wild.

"What are the deeper clues of who we are? Part of it has to do with our aspirations and our ideals, and part of involves subtle issues of integrity. Betrayals. All these darknesses. Being taken advantage of, losing money in the stock market, not being able to retire, wanting to live more of a creative life but having to make a living. Something means more than money. So, this curse of having to work for a living and not finding the work that you love: that could be a clue. That could be it. Who are we really?" asks George.

George gets to the bottom of self-discovery through a series of questions and answers. He doesn't hit people with it at first. But soon into the financial planning process, George will ask three questions to get an idea of the person he is working with.

"The first question that I ask is very much a money question: 'If you had all the money that you needed, what would your life look like?'

"Almost always the client will answer that question. 'Well, this is what I'd like, and this is what I'd like, and this is what I'd like.' And it's kind of all material, because you've got all the money. So, they dream about the houses and the vacations and what their work life would look like, or maybe they wouldn't work at all, and they tell you these things. Which is great. So, they've begun to open up and share their dreams and aspirations, and if you're a good listener, and you've been there for them, they're ready for the second question, which is this:

"If you went to the doctor this afternoon, and the doctor said 'I know you came in feeling perfectly healthy and everything, but here's the fact: You have a rare disease and the thing is that you'll never feel bad, but the bad news is that sometime between five and ten years from now you're just going to keel over dead.' And so the question that I have for you now is, 'How would that change your life? What would you do?'

"Suddenly, what happens in the room is that there is more of a hush. The person has already started to look at what they really want out of life. Now, this goes deeper, and there's a whole layer from that first question that just gets stripped away, that's superficial. But they still have their travel, and they have the home, and they still have their certain set of things that they'd still have. But it's stripped down, and it's gotten much more meaningful.

"Then there's the third question, and you've set them up so they've gone deeper now. So, you go to the doctor and the doctor says you have a very rare disease again, and I'm sorry to say you will be dead within twenty-four hours. So the question is, 'What did you miss?' 'What did you not get to do?' 'Who did you not get to see?' And there: really poignant stuff comes up. And there you might get the 'security' answer or the 'happiness' answer—'I never found happiness.' Different things come out."

I find myself, of course, running through the questions. What grandeur would I immediately flock to if money were no object? What do I really want to accomplish? What would I regret?

It's only the answers to the second and third questions that really matter, George says. "The other stuff is peripheral."

George's work is on connecting with the soul. He has found lots of other kindred spirits in the financial planning community. They have gotten together under the banner of Nazrudin (sic). And they have a Web site: *www.nazrudin.org.*

The mission that George and his cohorts are on is a big one.

"It was sex in the Sixties, and death in the Seventies, and now it's money. It's not easy, but it's meant to be something that teaches us and something that we recognize as part of our soul's journey."

Part of our soul's journey. Our soul's journey. It echoes. How often do we think of the soul?

"If people don't answer those things, they are going to die with regrets. We can come back to 'what does happiness mean?' and 'what does security mean in your life?' And we can attack it and put a dollar sign around it. And that's where we can help.

"So, you go down deep inside the soul and then you come back out and you try and make them connected. And the horrible thing is that we've split the thing in two. We've split the soul of the world in two. So that so many people will say that my spiritual life is great and my family life is wonderful, but it's my money life that sucks. And I know that when someone says that they have problems with their soul it's because money is meant to be an avenue, a pathway in which we express ourselves in the world. It's not always easy—in fact it's the toughest one of all."

The dark and fiery images that George sketches in his description of the soul aren't all that obtuse. He drills in a beat from Dante's Inferno, a reference to Milton. Somehow, it all fits into the context of money. "Dante's Inferno was full of money images," he notes.

But it's not the images. It's not the analysis. It's the suffering. I imagine that George has thought of this: that we can attach suffering to pretty much every-thing we do.

"This structure of suffering itself—how suffering gets hooked by the grasp-ing self. How to unlock that suffering of 'I,' 'me,' 'my' stories and relationships that get hooked to suffering. We can get trapped in a relationship with money that goes forever."

Divorcing from our programmed self is the impossible feat. But it's a jour-ney, to be sure.

"I tend to think that where we're headed is toward more meaning . . . and more and more toward letting go of structures of suffering so we can find more meaning.

"As long as we're sort of obsessed about money, and we're just there for the pursuit of it, there is a lack of a deeper meaning and a lack of understanding of who we are and of peace. And when we do those three questions, we come to those types of responses as opposed to the grasping of more money."

Those types of responses are grounded in awareness.

"There are three areas of awareness," George says. Clearly, he does like numbers.

"One: aspirations and ideals. The most powerful way to stimulate vigor is to help a client keep their eyes on the prize. What is the prize?

"Two: integrity. One of the main challenges money throws at us is the challenge to be aware of the violation of integrity around money, and what that will cost internally. To the extent that we violate ourselves around money, the more tendency to see the world as corrupt. Then, our intimate relationships are hardened. So, when you get very deep into your practice and you're on the verge of a big awakening, all your demons come up. So, if you have places that are really not understood by you where you've taken advantage, it's going to block your capacity for real awakening.

"Three: emotional responses. To observe emotions around money, interactions. Do they get hooked to these moments of guilt, shame, and humiliation of greed? And what's the 'I,' 'me,' and 'my'? What kind of messages come out? What are the 'I,' 'me,' and 'my' messages? What's the feeling that is uncomfortable?"

Finding peace is where George is leading. Peace takes a great deal of compassion for the self, that lonely person within who has no one to talk to but you.

What is he saying that he really wants? What is he saying that he would really regret?

Money may not be his only means of escape.

Dialogue: Me and My Imagination

"So I assume your were writing about me there?"

"It slipped out."

"I don't just manifest myself with money images, you know. There are other things I attach myself to. And certainly all this talk of suffering is lost on me."

"George skipped past the imagined self and hit chords more akin to the logical, reasoned self. So perhaps his points weren't so much directed at you but at the true self."

"You mean you."

"Yes, me. I, here, now, in the present, suffer much more than you imagine we suffer. It's I who has to deal with the hard facts, the hard lessons. I have to sign my name on checks to pay bills every month. I have to show up to work every day. I have to read and research and grow smarter. I have to try and actually do more. I can't always use your means of escape to create happiness in those moments, which I know—because I'm experiencing them—aren't happy moments. You're part of my world of fantasy. But the real world is full of pain and suffering."

"You have to admit that I make it better."

"Yes, you make it better when things aren't as good as they can be in the moment. Of course I turn to you, my faculty of imagination, to impute some sense of hope. Otherwise, I'd be living in despair. If I thought things were as good as it gets today, I wouldn't be happy."

"I never imagined."

"You must have imagined some *reason for existence* for yourself."

"Actually, no. I've only imagined various existences for you. I never even began to imagine the impetus for me to imagine those scenarios."

"I'm not saying that it's all bad all the time. But life is tough. It would be unbearable without you."

"Unless you had all the things you needed."

"But that's the point. We never can have all the things we need, because you end up designing more and more needs."

"Oh, so now you're going to blame all this pain and suffering on me, eh?"

"No blames. It's a fact. Desire falls under your domain. And we can never satiate all our desires."

"Who says? Can't we try? Isn't that what life is all about? If we have no desire, we have no reason to live."

"I think you may be confusing desire with hope."

"Hope, to me, seems very removed. It's like there is very little chance you'll ever get what you hope for. But desire—well, desire I can see getting."

"Of course you can because those things are past our needs. When we're blinded by needs, hope and desire seem very far removed, as you put it."

"So, you're saying that I don't exist on the very primitive level of need?"

"I, for one, can't remember you being around when I was just a child."

"That may be just a result of poor memory, because I certainly was there. You may not have used me very much, but I was there with big ears on until you decided to put me to good use."

"So, you're saying that imagination sleeps in the young and the needy, ready and waiting—for what?"

"For that day when hope enters the picture. Somehow, someway, hope enters. Then I recall all those desires—I imagine them and ways to get them. That's hope."

CHAPTER 13

The Poorest People In the World

Hope is hidden here. Hope is wrapped in the most basic of desires: food and shelter. Hope here is simply living.

I'm here in Ethiopia to investigate what money means to people in the poorest country in the world. And Ethiopia is the poorest country in the world, with the average person making just $100 per year.

I'm riding on a bus. Outside, I see fields bordered by shacks, bordered by buildings in disrepair. Everywhere, people are walking. They aren't orderly, rather they walk through the fields, across the roads, scattering like ants. It's as though an alarm has sounded, and every one is scurrying to get back inside their homes. They walk in a self-determined manner. "There is a place to get to and I'm going to get there," they might be thinking.

Old women carry stacks of firewood on their backs. Boys and girls taunt and chase each other, knocking into older people who seem to be heading to the office, the store, or the market. Cars careen through crowds. Pedestrians gingerly step out of the way just before, it seems, they are going to be run over. Autos don't take direction too well here. It's the person on foot who musters caution. Even on the long roads, where the buses go by at perilous speeds, people step—just so—out of the way. Even on the long roads past the city to the desert, people are walking.

This is the movement of Ethiopia.

In Ethiopia, "there are so many problems," says Surjit Singh, an economist and lead operations officer at the World Bank office in Addis Ababa, Ethiopia's capital city. Political: border clashes with neighboring countries, Eritrea and Somalia. A new government slowly disjoining from its Communist past. Agricultural: droughts, lack of reserves, poor transportation, cumbersome harvesting techniques. Economic: Prohibitive tariffs, massive debts, lack of a formalized and functioning infrastructure. Societal: Life expectancy of just forty-two years; 7.5 percent AIDS rate, projected to explode to upwards of 50 percent; intertribal warfare.

"Where do we begin?" Singh asks.

Singh is seated in a conference room in a modern-enough office building. Next to it, a family lives on the street. Across the road, young beggars play. Singh sighs. He and his staff sound almost defeated when speaking of Ethiopia's troubles—they're more than money can fix.

Money in Ethiopia isn't the same as money in most other places; it's the difference between life and death, having basic needs fulfilled—or not. Still, people don't kill for it. It's not a dangerous country.

Singh explains: "Rich live next to poor. There is no class system. In Kenya, for example, it's very dangerous, because there is a very distinct line—there are rich sections and there are poor sections. Here, everyone lives next to each other."

Everyone lives next to each other in the city. In the desert and the valleys where famine strikes, there are no neighbors to turn to. Everyone is affected in the same way. Most serious is the weather.

Droughts bring famine. Millions of people are displaced. It happens over and over. Herds die, crops fail. In the mid 1980s, Live Aid brought with it pictures of starving Ethiopian children in the desert. The song "We Are The World" was played over film footage of famine victims. Provocative displays of relief camps, masses of people lined up to receive food. Food drops from airplanes.

But this isn't how Ethiopia looks.

Addis Ababa is like a small town, except it's home to some 5 million people. There are office buildings and hotels, but imagine these are rundown—by Western standards, anyway. The worst section of any city conjures handily. Then, take it down a notch. Shanties, fashioned by strips of aluminum siding patched together by mud, line many of the roads.

Mostly, the main roads aren't paved. Street urchins mill amongst the constant flow of pedestrians. To be sure, some people are dressed in suits and ties, women in skirts. But the backdrop of religion exemplifies itself in most of the outfits that pass by: turbans, veils, the odd burnous, scarves, headdresses.

Ethiopia is half Islamic and half Christian, though ask any of either and they'll tell you they are the majority.

Cars are soiled, dented, ride on bald tires. Vans used as minibuses are jam-packed with riders.

And then there are the children. They swarm you. They carry things, anything—a newspaper, tissue, the odd trinket. These they try to sell you. Those that carry nothing just beg. They gesticulate the opposite of a kiss blown in the air. They hold out their hands and then close their fingers tight, together, as they bring them to their mouths. "Food," they are saying with their sad eyes. "I am hungry."

This is how Ethiopia looks.

The chants of the Coptic prayers wake me. They also put me to sleep. In the mornings, I hear these chants, like a Muslim's call to prayer, along with the sounds of runners' feet hitting the road. Before daybreak, I can see from my hotel room balcony the blur of colors flash by at dawn. Ethiopians are world-class runners, and students train and train for competition. They run in groups, one after the other, in the dark. Later, their footsteps will be traced over by the pedestrians on their way to work. Then, it is light outside.

At the Marcato, Africa's largest market of fruits, clothes, vegetables, and lots of other goods, an eerie quiet is brought forth from the bustle. Shoulder to shoulder, elbow to elbow, trades are conducted. The bargainers' singsong tune takes on a melody that rises and falls in harmony, so much so that you don't notice the sounds at first. It becomes quiet, like background noise again. Then the children break through. They chant: "Money! Money! Money!"

This is how Ethiopia sounds—quiet and melodic except for those words: "Money! Money! Money!" The children beg, "Hey mister. Hey you! Money! Money! Money!"

To be sure, Ethiopia is not what I imagined. It's more desperate. It's more desperate because its problems are ongoing. Isolated relief efforts would probably be welcome. But people live in poverty and go hungry every day. Even in the city. Even people with jobs. A college-educated woman who works at a hotel in Addis says that most of the people she knows go without at least one meal per day. Most.

Still, Ethiopia is changing. Relatively wet seasons have spawned better crops. People can farm, raise cattle, eat. New irrigation systems make this last.

I investigate the spots where food was air-dropped fifteen years ago to prevent millions from starving. I go to the desert. I visit the nomads who inhabit this part of Ethiopia. They admit that conditions are far better.

Relief workers say it's because they are moving from giving direct aid to development. Tamirat Yirgu, a worker at WorldVision, one of the largest relief agencies operating in the country, says, "When we just gave them the food and the assistance, there was no incentive for them to do anything else; they would just lay back. Now we are creating schools, developing irrigation programs, teaching them how to sustain their lives and maintain themselves."

Hope is leading the change.

"Although it's very difficult to have hope in this country," says Tamirat.

Signs abound. Sheik Al-Almoudi, a billionaire on the Forbes 400 list, is pouring huge amounts of money into the country. He has a brewery, a Pepsi distributorship, mining operations, and has built a world-class, five-star hotel in Addis Ababa.

My Imagination had a difficult time with this one. I'd even blurt: I can't imagine a hotel in such as place as this. But it's there.

The Sheraton Addis is an enormous 328-room hotel. All marble (90 percent Ethiopian) and gold (twenty-four-karat), it rivals any five star hotel I've seen in the world. At least five restaurants, numerous fountains, gold-inlaid columns and ceilings. It's tasteful, like a souped-up Four Seasons, and grand, like a Las Vegas hotel.

What's spooky: Not many people were staying at the Sheraton Addis, at least when I was there. A few African businessmen and Westerners roamed about, had cocktails in the lounge. For the most part, the restaurants were empty.

And during a day tour, after leaving the city street, shaking off the children who surrounded you with their chants, their attempts to get "Money! Money! Money!" you wonder, of course, why it's there. Just being on the hotel's meticulously manicured grounds, you feel guilty. There is a vast dichotomy between the world a few steps away and the world you are in.

"I can't stay there," said a woman from Vermont who works with local Ethiopian adoption agencies to bring children to the United States. "I feel too guilty."

Indeed, that is one way to think of it. But ask an Ethiopian whether the hotel is, well, too much, and they say, "No, it gives us hope."

The Sheik, a Saudi Arabian whose mother was Ethiopian, is creating jobs. The Sheraton Addis, for example, employs 650 people. His gold mines and other business ventures are also local, bringing even more people into the workforce.

"The Sheik," says Hagos Araya, an Ethiopian who works at the World Bank, "is a simple man. I see him at the "cafés". He is nice, approachable. We like what he is doing."

There is a yellow Corvette convertible parked at the entrance of the Sheraton Addis. It's the Sheik's. My Imagination envisions the Sheik, top down, cruising the streets of Addis. Children run up to his car. He showers them with money. He goes to the cafés, and people flock. He is smiling all the way, past the muddied shanties, the dirtied and soiled mothers holding even more dirtied and soiled children, curled up on the sidewalk, too weak to stand and even beg.

He may even take one of the children for a ride in his car. The child may put on a pair of sunglasses, be the envy of all of his friends. At the end of the ride, the Sheik may tell him to work hard and "one day, he too can have a car like this."

That is the message being displayed—capitalism at work in its most embryonic of stages. People are embracing it.

The song "Survivor" by the group Destiny's Child blares out the window of this small minibus. A boy, literally, is spilling out the window. Twenty of us cram into this sorry vehicle meant for twelve. Islamic symbols adorn the front windshield: the symbol of Allah, with its backwards "P," laminated verses from the Koran, Fatiha.

It's a blue and white VW, bus and it's dented. The tires are bald. Muslim dress mixes with Western outfits. We drive fast. Thumps on the door mean stop. Thumps on the door mean go. We pass goat herders, woman walking with piles of firewood on their backs, donkeys toting you name it.

The "Survivor" song gets louder as we drive through the center of Addis. Lacking are billboards or posters or advertising. Sure there are a few, but not many. No cell phones, no infusion of technology or pop culture that stand out.

This is basic. People walk. They talk in person. They don't meet at cafés or restaurants. They don't go shopping at malls or spend evenings watching television.

The luxuries that would support anything more aren't there. Money for that can't be spent yet. Money has to be invested in infrastructure and programs to provide for the basic needs, then sweeteners will follow. Now it's just survival.

Ethiopia sits at the eastern most tip of Africa, referred to as the Horn. It has a total population of 58 million. The country has never been colonized, except for a brief period of Italian rule.

There is something more to it. The country's history is as poignant as its current conditions. It's intriguing, maddening, compelling, curious.

Ethiopia is home to Lucy, the oldest-known human ancestor. It allegedly houses the famed Ark of the Covenant, where the tablets on which the Ten Commandments are written, are stored. It's home to Queen Sheba, Emperor Haile Selassie, or Ras Tafari. It traces histories back so far, it's known as the Cradle of Humanity. But the irony is evident is every sense of that meaning—humanity.

In the first millennium A.D., Ethiopia was among the most powerful kingdoms in the world. Its center was Aksum, an ancient city in the northern part of the country (where the Ark is still supposedly stored). Its influence spread across the Red Sea to southern Arabia. It was rich, advanced; it minted coinage in bronze, silver, and gold. It embraced Christianity (even inscribing the cross on its coins, the first people in the world to do so). Then, followers of Islam came to Ethiopia. The Arabs were growing in power and fortunes. Aksum's influence waned. Coins even ceased to be minted. It all curiously went silent. Money evaporated. Barter came back into existence with salt, iron, or cloth. And then the Muslim-Christian wars broke out. Churches were burned, thousands killed. The country split into tribes. This lasted until the nineteenth century, when Kassa Haylu, a virtual Robin Hood, began to steal from the rich and give to the poor. He united the nation once again and was named Emperor Tewodros.

Just when things got settled, the British invaded and robbed the country of its treasures and left. Then the Italians stepped in under Mussolini's famous campaign to colonize the country. Bloody battles ensued. Italy lost more than 4,000 soldiers, Ethiopia 275,000 people.

Through it all, however, Ethiopia refused to be ruled.

The ruler of today's Ethiopia is money. Its ideological past is being buried. People like Sheik Almoudi are being joined by wealthy Westerners with a cause. Philip Berber, who sold his company Cybercorp to Charles Schwab & Co. for $500 million, has set up a $100 million foundation that strictly invests in Ethiopia.

Berber says, "This is an entrepreneurial, nonbureaucratic, cost-effective, highly accountable approach to international aid. We have a $100 million fund, and we redistribute the interest and funds arising from that to help relieve some of the pain and suffering on the planet. And, because we are not spending the principal sum itself, we'll still have $100 million creating interest and capital to invest in projects next year and for the next seven generations."

Berber joins the mantra: help people who are helping themselves. The World Bank is counting on such a system of self-governance and self-sustainability. It has changed its monetary assistance to poverty-reduction programs. These new initiatives tie debt relief to development programs in poor nations. So, instead of retired debt going toward, say, military spending, the World Bank is requiring those monies to be allocated to specific development programs. This requires Ethiopia's government to comply with World Bank initiatives. It requires oversight, monitoring, and participation—things not so easily accomplished in a continent prone to political instability and corruption.

But trickle-down is the hope.

The rains in Ethiopia come between July and October. They come in floods. And sometimes they don't come back. Then, the dry land makes farming impossible. People begin to starve and die of thirst. They then herd together. Relief camps are set up, and the world sometimes watches.

Word trickles out, people need help. Money is given. People live. It's the most direct impact and most powerful result money can provide.

Standing on the ground where food was air-dropped fifteen years ago by the Live Aid campaign is a young girl. She is nine. Shy to speak, she grabs the hem of her dirty purple dress and looks down. Her family are semi-nomadic—they wander where they can to find food. A new irrigation system, backed by a $70,000 investment from World Vision may allow her to stay and attend school; her family can tend crops. Through an interpreter, she's asked her dream.

"To be a teacher," she says, "or an investor."

You can bet she doesn't know what a stock or a bond is. She's not talking about investing, as we know it, for money. She's talking about investing as she knows it—in herself, in her land, in her people.

Close by, a man, perhaps fifty years old, is standing in a field. He is rough-skinned. He wears a loose white turban, but his clothes are Western—an open-collared shirt, cotton chino pants. He is dirty, thin, and walks using a stick. He says he used to shepherd goats, but now he is learning to farm.

He's asked what money means to him. He says it will allow him to increase the size of his field; he can grow more crops.

And what if he had all the money he could ever want?

It's beyond him. He cannot think that way. He's like a prisoner who only focuses on getting through that day. Hopes and dreams and thoughts of an outside world, a better place, are prescriptions for going mad. Such thoughts breed inexorable feelings of depression, despair—the lack of hope.

The man says simply, "I don't have such grand visions. I am a simple farmer. I just want to be able to feed my family. That is enough."

Within view sits an abandoned palace. It's high on a hill in the range that overlooks this valley. It was built as an imperial palace retreat.

Wouldn't you like to have that? Live up there in that palace?

"That," he says "has its own requirements."

A different life. A different set of values.

Rough terrain through unpaved roads. Dust flies in our wake. Round, straw huts dot the path to the main road ahead. Women, whose faces are tattooed in demarcations of beauty—a cross, the symbol of a female; ♀,—stand and watch us pass by. Along their necks are stripes or polka dots. More symbols, more signs tattooed on them.

A mother of three who lives in one of these one-room huts, twelve feet by twelve feet in size, says she is happy. She wants nothing more.

"I have my husband, my children. I am taken care of," she says, and smiles. "What more could I want? I have all that I need."

Her children are held in awe of our cameras. They want nothing but to look inside our car.

Appreciation takes many forms, from the simplest to the most complex.

I still imagine the children chanting, except for one. He was the boy who rode in the yellow Corvette with the Sheik. He is working to relive that day, that impossible, unimaginable day, when he drove through the streets like a king and was given hope.

Dialogue: Me and My Imagination

"I don't know if I like where this is going."

"Why is that?"

"Seems depressing. I mean, sure, people have hope there. We've established that. Good news for the likes of me. It doesn't mean that you need money to be imaginative. But the reality is that they can't put me to as much use as you can."

"Because they don't have the exposure to new things or the luxury of exploring and creating."

"Right. When you're rich, you can imagine more because you're exposed to more."

"Ah, but there's the rub. Then you might slacken, see. Once good, old reality actually takes hold of you and makes what you've dreamed up—a fact—you're obsolete."

"I hadn't thought about it that way."

"Indeed. On the very basic level of need, there is nowhere to go but up."

"Hmm. The Sheik does seem to be having fun putting his imagination to work in Ethiopia."

"Right. And look at the richest country in the world. Know what it is?"

"You're the brains, I'm the bullshit, remember?"

" . . . well, you could imagine."

"Switzerland? Monaco? Some tiny place with lots of rich people?"

"Some tiny place with lots of rich people is right. Luxembourg."

"I imagined that was part of France."

"Whatever. Luxembourg it is. And you know what? Imaginations don't seem to be running wild there."

"Oh, yes—we've been . . . "

"Staid, boring. Banking is its big claim to fame. Wake up. "

"Yeah, yeah. Luxembourg. How exciting."

"Hardly. You wouldn't last long there—not that they'd want you."

"Rich people don't like change."

"Well, just as poor people have nowhere to go but up, rich people . . . "

"Yes, yes, I get it."

"You know, there is a slogan scrawled in quite a few places in Luxembourg: *Mir wëlle bleiwe wat mir sin*—'We want to remain what we are.'"

"That doesn't sound too friendly."

"Well, at least it's not a solicitor of change."

"So I imagine all the hope lies at the bottom."

"There is a big dichotomy there. And the problems begin to arise in the middle."

"Why?"

"Because that's when the rubber begins to hit the road. 'This is what I hoped for. This is how it's supposed to be,' and when it isn't, look out."

"That reality, she's a bitch."

"No kidding. A lot of people are mad at her and they take action."

"I'm imagining riots, rebellion, violence in general."

"Deeper, really. When people have a chance and they don't take it, or if they think someone else is taking it from them, they become bitter—sometimes, yes, violent. And you can replace chance with money or money with chance."

"I imagine that's where all those right-wing groups get their fuel—from missed opportunity."

"Or lost opportunity. Strangely, it's not just the right wing. It's the left wing too. Radical communists, as we write these words, are rioting in Genoa, Italy, protesting rich nations' policies. Someone, even, was just killed."

"I'm picturing police in riot gear waving batons and shields. Protesters in street clothes, thousands of them, throwing rocks, overturning cars, smashing windows."

"In this news piece, as I now read it, you're exactly right. The battle between rich and poor."

"So it's not right or left?"

"No. The money battle is waged on both sides—and even in the middle. The average person voices his or her agreement or disagreement with monetary policy by the way they vote."

"I imagine that's why a candidate, such as the one we just had, was able to win the presidency. Tell people they'll keep more of their money. Tell people they'll prosper. Ignite other imaginations like me out there. Let them run wild with possibilities."

"For the average person, you're right—that'll most likely win them over. But get this fact, and here's one that will keep you busy: Some super-wealthy Americans actually want to pay *more* taxes—or have less money, if you will."

"I can't imagine why."

"Because, they say if they're allowed to keep such hordes of capital, their offspring will have a leg up on society. They don't want that. They want to keep America's class and social system just the way it is. In fact, they're called United For a Fair Economy."

"A stingy, old man, some Ebenezer Scrooge–type has found friends, like himself, who would rather give money away to the government than to their own children?"

"Seems so. But they're not such odd characters as what you describe. The father of the richest man in the world is part of the group: Bill Gates, Sr."

"Of course, what does his kid have to worry about—"

"Eh, let me finish. So is a list of Who's Who billionaires: Warren Buffett, George Soros, Ted Turner. And lots of centimillionaires. These guys and gals represent the wealthiest 5 percent of the country. That's a pretty amazing display of support for leveling the economic game, don't you think?"

"Being built, as I am by you, I'm skeptical. I'd say there was a trick here. And I'm thinking tax break."

"No, no. This is a morality play. Plenty of people want to put hope back in the game. Plenty of rich people give up what they have and help others get a leg up in the world. They are the enlightened ones. They see a bigger picture. They imagine the world a better place for everyone."

"I take offense to that. I imagine the world a better place."

"For us."

"Well, mostly. We can't afford to be charitable yet."

"We're to busy running around trying to impress god-knows-who with what we have. We're trying to fulfill some need of security."

"And I imagine those who act so charitable, as you say, are also looking to fulfill a need?"

"Good point. But their needs actually help the needs of others. People like us, we're just selfish and self-involved."

"Show me someone who isn't."

"Some people can't afford to be. And some people choose to make a commitment to care."

"Listen, I saw all those relief workers in Ethiopia. We didn't get too spiri-
   tual."
"You mean they didn't walk around with a sign on, as you imagined,
   saying, 'Hey, look at me, I'm doing a good thing here.'"
"You're really starting to piss me off."
"Because you can't imagine how someone could be so needy, or because
   you can't imagine someone being so pure?"
"Both."
"Watch and learn."

CHAPTER 14

The Basic Determinants of Needs

The road is long. Deserted fields lay on each side. A farmhouse looms in the distance. Snow covers the fields. Patches of crusted ice and dirty snow are on the banks next to which he trots. He wears just a windbreaker, sneakers, jeans, and a light shirt. He has exactly $5 in his pocket. He has exactly $5, period.

It's gray, no matter what the time of day. His hands are red, even though most of the time he leaves them in his pockets as he walks. And he walks. Through Kansas. Missouri is far away from where he began. St. Joseph is where he lived. Joseph, the father of Jesus. Joseph, who is supposed to be the protector. Yes, that Joseph. A small town in Missouri has taken his name. But Joseph was nowhere to be found that night—how many nights ago he can't even remember—when he left that place.

Only one truck has stopped to give him a lift. He fears sleeping on the side of the road; it's too cold and he might not wake. Better to walk on.

"George," he tells me his name, proud as punch. He's just removed his graduation gown and cap. He's standing now in a suit and tie. "Just got my GRE." Five foot four or five, George shows the signs of a difficult life—tough skin, hard wrinkles, eyes that have long lost the ability to see hope in anything or anyone. Brown hair cut, perfunctorily groomed. George is forty-two. He is homeless. He lives at the Denver Rescue Mission, one of the oldest homeless shelters in the country.

George walked and hitched from Missouri to get here. Not that this was the place he had intended; he was headed toward Modesto, California, to see his brother. "But I called, and he told me I wasn't much welcome," says George. "Thank God for that."

The Denver Rescue Mission has been his home for close to nine months. He's sober now, earns his keep, is studying hard to go on to a college where he can study computers. "If I could just get that algebra," he says.

The balance of equations George studies now are of a different type. Moving from the Northwest to the South with a woman he met. Trying to care for her two children. Hanging on to that security until that fateful night. Until she couldn't take it anymore. Until she couldn't take George anymore. So, maybe he had had a few too many. Maybe he had had too much anger. "And I could see red," he says. Maybe he had done what men had been taught not to do. Maybe he had had enough of repressing the violence and the rage of being abandoned as a child, separated from his natural brother, being raised by stepparents who might not have cared so much. Maybe that all rose to the surface one fateful night in Missouri when Saint Joseph lapsed in his role as protector and George had his chance to lash out. Maybe.

Walking to California in the bitter cold with just $5 in his pocket must surely have been better than living with the results of his actions, her actions, their life.

My Imagination can see George on that long road in Kansas. He can see that farmhouse, which is now close. A quick right turn into the driveway, and George will be there. The wood is piled high on the side of the house. Smoke is billowing out the chimney. Warmth. Comfort. A place to eat or spend the night.

"But I was afraid I'd scare someone and get into more trouble," says George.

So he walks past the driveway. The gray sky won't admit whether it's morning or afternoon. The long road ahead doesn't bend. It's a straight path. George doesn't know where that will take him, but it's a direction. He has no choice but to take it. Finally, a car stops there and then leaves him here, right out front. An omen. The people at the Denver Rescue Mission take him in. They welcome him in. And it's warm.

Brad Mueli is the director of the Denver Rescue Mission. He sees a lot of men like George come and go. It isn't money troubles that leave people like George at the Mission's door; it's life troubles.

Brad can testify to money's place in these people's lives. As a former vice president of a major bank, Wells Fargo, Brad has helped many people with money issues. But here, it's not like that.

"It impacts every part of my life. It impacts my entire being. It impacts everything you do," he says. "As a banker, there are only so many Mercedes you can take from those home equity loans. Here, we're giving people something very different."

Brad says he won't tell me until the end of our discussion what that something is. He wants me to spend the day, meet the people, the staff, see for myself what the Mission is all about.

"A lot of people have come up to me and said, 'I wish I had the courage to do what you're doing.' A lot of people want to do good things," he says.

But make no mistake, it takes courage. Brad has five children, ranging in age from twenty-two to eight years old. Two of his kids are in college. "We had to have a discussion about our change in lifestyle," Brad says. "But it really hasn't been so much; it's different. Sure, I don't make what I used to, and money is tight. But I have so much more now."

Brad says it's the people who make the difference. He says, "These guys, they're at the bottom rung. And sometimes, I am sitting there and having a conversation and I forget their situation, forget that they're homeless. You come to realize, they're just real people like you and me."

Brad introduces me to a large black man named Gilbert. "He'll show you around," says Brad.

Gilbert is one of those fellows who reminds you of a big, gentle bear. Something about him is soft. I figure that since he is a Rescue Mission staffer, he must have worked himself up from the street. There's something shy and humble about him.

We sit on little plastic chairs in the chapel, where Gilbert tells me that services are held every day. "Mandatory for residents," he says. About 110 people live at the Denver Rescue Mission. But Christianity isn't force-fed. "We have Muslims, Buddhists, Jewish guys. This is more of a place to show respect than a house of worship," Gilbert says.

But Gilbert is a Christian. He was active in his local church in Detroit, leading the choir. "I would sing, direct, teach music," he recalls. For the first time, Gilbert's eyes slide from mine. He takes a handkerchief from his pocket and dabs his forehead. "I was married," he says.

His stepson began selling drugs in the house. His wife became a drug addict. He began to drink. They divorced. But the seed had been planted in Gilbert. He moved to Denver, met another woman, married her, was beginning to turn things around. "Then she asked me for a divorce too," he says, dabbing again. A white woman, she couldn't handle the "cultural differences," he says. "That devastated me—to the point where I fell and didn't want to get back up.

"I didn't want to get back up to fall again. I was working two jobs to support my habit. Then I lost them."

Down and out, Gilbert had lost two toes loading a truck on a day job. He couldn't function, couldn't pay for medical expenses. He turned for help.

He said to himself, "Change needs to happen, or this is going to be the place you'll be for the rest of your life."

Gilbert is careful with his words. He'll take long pauses between sentences. He wants to get it right. For example, he says you hope for things to be different—not better—when you're down and out.

"Better is what may have been destructive in our lives. Once you come into a place of a fall, money becomes a support of your habit. And that you'll have until you change your mind. We feel like we need to work and have money in our lives. But when you're using it to destroy your life—"

At this, he trails off. He doesn't complete the sentence. Instead, he looks away.

"I had those things," he says, softly. "Money can be a way of getting things, but until you get to that place of stability within you to make a change, to offer gifts you have on the inside . . . those gifts on the inside you can get without money . . . money is destructive."

Gilbert's point: Money supports the bad system of habits that entails self-destruction. Until you can change the system, money only perpetuates the destructive behavior.

"It keeps you longer in you weakness," he says.

No one seems to miss money here, where shelter and food are provided free of charge. New Mission residents are given $10 per week. After three years, a resident gets $15 per week. Graduates get a car and part of their rent paid.

I'm back in Brad's office, where he tells me the two biggest reasons for homelessness are lack of transportation and rent rates.

"We try and make it as easy as possible to remove the financial pressures as well," Brad says.

"Yes," I reply, "Gilbert, your staff director, told me."

"Gilbert? He is a phase three resident. He's not on staff, he's one of the homeless we've taken in."

"But, he's so . . ."

"Normal?" Brad asks. "Yes, that is the something I was talking about. They have self-respect. That's something most of them never had before."

I praise Brad. "It's great," I find myself saying. "You're giving people so much."

"Giving? I don't look at it as giving. I'm the one who's been blessed by this whole deal."

I leave Brad's office and make my way down the stairs toward the front entrance. Dozens of homeless people have begun to spill in, lining up for a free lunch. In the cafeteria, a family of five takes up a whole table, the young children run to the food. A straggly man in a dark hat and glasses stands in a corner, brooding. Some are dirty. Some are clean.

The room fills up, and I leave.

A small handmade flyer is tacked to the door: IT'S NEVER TOO LATE TO START DOING WHAT IS RIGHT.

The average age of the people at the homeless shelter is forty-one.

Outside, the rains that have continued nonstop in Denver for two weeks end. The sun begins to shine.

I know now what that "something" is that Brad spoke about, that he wouldn't tell me at the beginning of our conversation. What he and his staff give the homeless people who turn to them for help is a sense of self-worth. And that has nothing to do with money.

Dialogue: Me and My Imagination

"It's easy for me, you know."

"What's that?"

"Skidding off the map, getting us down and out. I can easily imagine these things."

"It's certainly a big fear. It's why I tap away so much on this keyboard. It's why I constantly configure scenarios of doom. I've even begun to think that that's what keeps us going."

"The dire images you have me conjure you really believe will become a reality?"

"In a sense. What would become of us if we didn't do this, or do that."

"I can't imagine that ever really happening."

"Because of you, I suppose."

"Programmed, might I remind you, by you. Reality, the world you live in, needs me to do more than just fantasize. I'm here to imagine new heights, prevent us from falling to new lows. It's an upward climb, I tell you."

"And you are imagining that you are the elevator that lifts us."

"If you're to be so perfunctory as to use ups and downs, highs and lows, I suppose, yes. I prefer to imagine in a different way."

"Which is?"

"A helix explanation to life, a matrix that pushes and pulls, ebbs and flows."

"But that must begin with some basic foundations—food, shelter. Then love and belonging, or security. With such solidity of mind, we can move forward toward putting our ego into play, heading toward what will make us, in the end, happy."

"And I've imagined—and I think you've so far proven—that money is the ultimate promulgator toward that end."

"From your perspective, still, maybe. From mine, money isn't the proven solution."

"Ah, yes. That's what you've been stuck on. Let me hand you a little something I use quite frequently—actions, verbs, movement. You seem to use money as a noun. Try using it as an active noun—or even a verb, for that matter. It gets us places, places I conjure."

"So you could equate a lack of imagination with being poor."

"I've always imagined it that way. Look at some of the most creative people we know. Do they lead 'better' lives than some of the richest people we know?"

"Most, well, yes."

"They can do more with what they've got. It's not about the money. It's about living well."

"Indeed, I look around us here in Positano, Italy. The house where John Steinbeck created the most, or so he said, is just over there. It looks out on to the sea. Below his balcony, a woman selling sarongs and beach sandals sits happily in the shade, fanning herself. The cliffs reach high into the clouds. Sun breaks through the crests in late morning. Light refracts beneath the wake of yachts that moor or simply cruise by, creating the most illuminating blue-green. A hat, a book, a bathing suit is all that is needed to achieve a sense of happiness. In fact, I'm immensely happy now. Put me in New York, and things would be different."

"Because I imagine a different sense of happiness. Here, it's simple for me—and therefore for you. I only have a few elements to work with here. Happiness is just the fulfillment of basic needs, the surrounding takes care of the rest—the sea and those cliffs you spoke of."

"That's why artists like it here. You can be put to better use, or something other than everyday use, anyway. There's a bigger sense of fulfillment, too."

"Yeah 'cause I have a mission. I have a world to create. There isn't enough of one here."

"We shrink enough away from the real world and your power grows substantially."

"But we get along nice enough, yeah?"

"Sure, you get your way most of the time. There's a danger in that, you know."

"I imagine you're thinking of all those artists who realized the two worlds could never join."

"Hence all those suicides. A shame."

"And you? I've had to imagine those circumstances as well. Usually when you're quite down."

"Brings us full circle, no? How far are those at the absolute top of
Maslow's hierarchy from those at the absolute bottom? And how
much does money make a difference?"

"I suppose I'd have to be exposed to having it all, from self-esteem on
down."

"Sort of what I was thinking."

"Because we think alike"

"But how do we get to the next level of love and belonging? I mean, I
can see how we can survive by fulfilling the basic needs. But how do
we step up?"

"In the context of money, it's getting it."

"And how do we do that?"

"There are only a few ways to get money: earn it, steal it, win it, or inherit
it. Whether any of those leads to having a sense of love and belonging
is a whole other question."

"Which I imagine we're about to try and answer."

"You said it."

CHAPTER 15

Self-Worth

Marlene just got off welfare. She's making $5 per hour, just scraping by. Two kids and rent. Two kids and rent.

"One paycheck away," she says, from being back, from being down and out. "It's not easy. That's the fear." She washes dishes at a restaurant.

No education. No skills. The beat rolls on, the crowd rolls over her. She isn't down and out anymore—she's a mishap away. And that may be scarier.

"Now, at least, I have something. If I lose that, I don't know what I'd do. When I had nothing, it didn't matter. Now it does."

Sure, it does. She's like millions of Americans. One step away from being on the street. With a zero savings rate in the United States, Marlene isn't alone. But it's tough to find love and belonging when worries are on your mind.

Do I even need to describe Marlene? She could be black, white, Hispanic, Chinese. She could be Jewish, Christian, Muslim, agnostic, atheist. She could be fat, skinny, ugly, pretty, tall short.

None of the physical features of Marlene matter. None of the religious systems matter. Not even her name matters.

What matters most to Marlene is money. That will give her self-esteem. That will give her the sense of security she needs.

Two children grab on to her legs. They are cute. They are happy. They play in the street. They run to Marlene.

"I have just enough," she says. "Just enough for the basics."

That rules out treats like ice cream and candy. It rules out family vacations or trips to the zoo. It means no video games or cable. For her, there's no decision of which restaurant to eat at. There's no contemplation of what to do with leisure time. "Those things costs money, money I just don't have," says Marlene.

Okay Marlene. So who are you? How did you get to be the person you've become? How come earning money is so important to you?

"Earning money is my only means of escape."

From a world that's not so good. From a world that means sacrificing some part of your morality to survive. From a world without hope.

"I grew up this way. I don't want my kids to, too."

Second-generation welfare. Government statistics show that most welfare recipients stay on the dole, go back on the dole, never break away from the system. The likelihood their children will go on welfare, too, is high.

"We didn't have anything."

But were you happy?

"No. No, I wasn't happy. If I was happy I wouldn't be doing this for them."

The kids stand there and poke each other in the doorway. A stranger has called. It's a treat. It's something, someone new. And it doesn't cost anything.

"Who are you? Where are you from? Why are you here?"

The questions rattle back and forth from me to them.

Should I mention who they are, where they're from, why they're here? Come on, Marlene, tell us.

Picture this: a father who can't hold down a job, a mother who is pregnant all the time. Picture this: a small, two-bedroom apartment, converted to three. Picture this: an apartment building, part of a city "project." Three towers rise high into the sky. They overlook nothing but the urban landscape. The elevators break a lot, and you have to walk up and down the stairs—all ten floors. Momma's pregnant again. You're the oldest. You have to help out. Picture this: shopping at secondhand clothes stores, turning in food stamps. Going hungry some days. Picture this: the cycle continuing, your family living that way.

No, no, it can't be. It has to stop with you. So, you get out as soon as you can.

Now this: no education. No formal training. Taken care of by a man who left. Forced onto the street. Family isn't around. But the welfare office is. Her friends do it, why shouldn't she? She's knows how. She knows the system. It's how she grew up. It's second nature.

"I'm no saint. I've made mistakes in my life," Marlene says. "But I want to work. I want to earn my keep."

Why? Because there's a better life. She's cognizant of that. Responsibility first. Recognition second. And move up the chain. Maybe it's as the cook. Maybe it's as the waitress. Maybe she could host or manage the place someday. Maybe she could even own her own business. It's the dream. It's the first step. It's where the imagination runs wild with hope.

Indeed, my Imagination conjures: Marlene drying off the last plate left in the sink. She flicks the hand towel over her shoulder. The last bubbles of suds disappear down the drain. She wipes the sweat from her brow and walks to the time clock where she'll punch out. But a man, a short man in a white short-sleeve shirt, tie, and glasses is standing there. He wears a nametag. It says MANAGER.

In the back he takes her, to his office. He sits behind a cheap, metal desk, piled high with manila folders. He takes off his glasses. He chats about the evening's business with Marlene, who is so tired, so god dammed tired, and wants nothing but to get home to her kids. He talks about a problem he's been having with an employee. And Marlene gets a lump in her throat. She thinks he may be speaking about her. She adjusts herself. She becomes uncomfortable. An anxious knot develops in her stomach. "What am I going to do? What am I going to do? What am I going to do?"

She is thinking rapid-fire as he talks. "A girlfriend knows about a job as a chambermaid . . . "

But he cuts into her thinking. "Would you consider . . . ?" he asks. " It will mean more money."

Her attention is fully on him now. She gasps. It all goes blank then fills into a wide smile. They shake hands.

And Marlene, light on her feet the whole way home, stops for the first time at the corner store and buys candy for her kids.

She's stepped up. Sweet, like that.

That's how it could happen. Not likely. But it *could*.

Writer Barbara Ehrenreich lived the life that the Marlenes of the world live. She spent two years working in minimum wage jobs across the United States. What did she find? The escape hatch was locked shut, battened down by the system, by managers and owners who held workers in their place; it's not worth their while to allow people like Marlene to have a leg up.

"Lousy pay makes for unlucky lives," Ehrenreich concluded in her book *Nickel and Dimed: On (Not) Getting By in America.* [9]

In an interview, Ehrenreich, who holds a doctorate in biology, said, "I think there is a certain kind of middle- and upper-middle-class complacency about the poor. People say, 'Oh yeah, they have a hard time, but they get by.'"

Sure, they get by.

But it's really, really hard. It's really, really tiring. It's really, really frustrating. And that's the sad lesson of earning too little. You can never earn enough.

So, what's the hope, what's the dream, what's the point?

Security, you see. Security that you'll have a roof over your head and food on your plate. Security that you can feed your family. For some, it's a long way off. For others, perhaps even more disturbingly, it's tantalizing.

"I can see it," says Marlene. "It's right in front of me."

But she can't get there—yet.

What Marlene has is imagination. She too puts him to work every day in search of hope. She too uses him to ward off reality and dream of a better day.

Money, for Marlene, is not having to worry about completing the "what ifs" of going without just one paycheck.

She's on the tightrope, where so many people walk. And money would be her safety net—just a little, and she plans to earn it.

Dialogue: Me and My Imagination

"There was a lot more to that story. I could have had some real fun there."

"We both could have—a book in itself. But that's not what we're here to do."

"Shutting me down at every turn?"

"Keeping you focused on money, its attachments, its meaning, its reason for existence."

"That's obvious so far. You can't help but imagine money will lead to a better life in those circumstances. I mean, that's basic."

"Don't you think that everyone at every stage wants a better life?"

"Little stuff, sure. But when I have to imagine ways to eat, to pay for shelter—that takes up a great deal of my time. After all that, I'd be too pooped to worry about travel and leisure."

"Perhaps that's just us."

"I imagine it's every one. There's that question that always wakes me, even when I'm in the deepest and darkest of slumbers: 'Wouldn't it be nice?' I can't help but to rise to the occasion."

"That's partially my fault, I'm afraid. When I'm not satisfied, that question pops into my mind. Sometimes the question is more vehemently asked, I grant you. But most of the time it's a little plaything: 'Oh, wouldn't that be nice?' It's a luxury. You don't ask yourself that when you are hungry. You ask yourself that when you're looking for a garnishment."

"I imagine, however, that some people may just be content with the meal as it is: the roasted chicken breast, mashed potatoes, string beans. Who needs the parsley anyway?"

"Well, isn't that what makes someone more sophisticated than another?"

"I make someone more sophisticated. I imagine all sorts of things to better a situation. And I'll tell you this: the more sophisticated, the more expensive. That's where money comes into the picture."

"I'm thinking of the intellect. I can have a more sophisticated point of view than someone else. That doesn't necessarily mean that I have more money."

"Intellect, schmintellect. The more you know, the more you want. Come, take a little tour with me, would ya, and I'll show you: Park Avenue in New York City. Both sides of the street are lined with yellow taxicabs, black Lincoln Town Cars—a horse and carriage trots by. It's fall. The leaves are changing color, but there is still enough green on the ground to brighten the median strip that runs down the center of the avenue. Elegantly dressed people are on their way home from work, or on their way out after work. They look as though they mingle on the sidewalk. Tailor-made suits for the gents. Designer-made dresses for the ladies. Couture. High fashion abounds. Now, let's follow one of them into one of those high-rise, luxury buildings that sits so grandly on either side of the street. You know the ones, with the green awnings that jet out to the curb. The ones where the doormen wear white gloves and neat, green and black uniforms.

"Inside, we walk past a heavy glass door to the marble lobby. A few plants. A brass bucket for umbrellas. No unseemly desk awaits. God knows where the doormen sit when no one is around. Surely it isn't on one of the needlepoint couches or leather chairs. Maybe they stand and look at the horse and hound tapestries. In any event, when the elevator man pushes back the door cage, a woman wearing a chinchilla fur wrap and sunglasses steps out and walks past us. We comment on the time of year, that it's too early for fur, to the elevator man, who, in like uniform as the doorman, takes us to the top floor. The door opens directly into a waiting area reserved for this apartment and this apartment only. It's starkly different than the clubby feel of the lobby. Beige Italian marble imported from the quarries just outside Siena; hand-grooved base-boards. The second door, just painted in a Ralph Lauren flat white, opens to the tri-level, four-thousand-square-foot apartment itself. Steel gray ceilings and walls float to doublewide, custom teak floors. On the walls: a small portrait of a dancer by Degas, a blue-period Picasso, the original Matisse sketch for a *Back* sculpture, and, for kicks, an Egon Schiele nude. A dining room set imported from Morocco, a living room featuring a down-filled custom couch upholstered with $1,000-per-yard French fabric. Viking appliances accentuate the kitchen. A wine collection includes a 1998 Chateau Le Pin, a 1990 Chateau Petrus, and a rare 1961 Bordeaux Carruades de Chat. Each bedroom has been sound-proofed. Still, a THX surround-sound system and Nakamichi stereo make the apartment media room buzz with classical music.

"We, or the person we've followed in from the street, are late for a fundraising event, so we drop our Cartier key chain into the Lalique bowl we use for such items. We undo our Hermes tie, slip off our Edward Greene loafers, unbutton our Ike Behar shirt, and unbuckle the A. Testoni belt as we remove it from the slips of our Zegna slacks. All this as we zip back to the bedroom, where we'll enter our own dressing room and change into a Brioni tuxedo with matching shirt and change our Rolex GMT Master II sport watch for a Patek Philippe chronograph. The cufflinks—Harry Winston mother of pearl set in platinum—go on easy, but tying the Turnbull & Asser bowtie, from a thick Indian silk weave, takes longer than we expected. On go the antique, hand-blown, German-made glass lights, off goes Bach's Cello Suite No. 3 in C Major (being performed by Pablo Casals) that has been playing. If we take a quick peek over the balcony we can see whether our Rolls-Royce Silver Seraph has arrived. And we exit the same way as which we came."

"You suppose that is better than living in a one-bedroom walkup, cracking open a can of beer and flopping on a Jennifer Convertible couch to watch a ball game?"

"I was making the point of knowing better. I don't use 'better' or 'worse' in an egotistical way; that's your job. I just produce the images you associate with better or worse. But I'll tell you one thing, what I described is more expensive. And, in the past, you've made me equate more expensive with better."

"We're coming back to that issue of 'satisfaction' again. Can people be satisfied with an average lifestyle? Does the car have to be the Mercedes? Can't it be a Honda? Do the clothes have to be designer-made?"

"From the information I'm exposed to, there is a certain cache equated with finer. A refined taste is better, or so you lead me to believe."

"But the average individual doesn't live that way. The typical American family, for example, makes $39,000 per year. They live outside major metropolitan areas, mostly in the suburbs. The father or mother, or both, commutes to an eight-hour-per-day job. They have one or maybe two children, own two (American-made) cars, have a pet, and take approximately two weeks of vacation per year."

"We mostly live in New York and Los Angeles. I can't imagine living that way."

"The statistics also show this: Upper-middle-class people live about the same way and make between $75,000 and $1 million per year. Rich people live pretty much the same way and make between $1 million and $10 million per year. It's only the super-rich, who earn more than $10 million per year, who live life dramatically differently. Dinesh D'Souza, in his fine book *The Virtue of Prosperity*,[10] quotes these statistics and says, 'rich people can do whatever they want within reason, but they cannot do whatever they want, period. That honor belongs to the super-rich.'"

"So how am I supposed to imagine that the typical American family is happy when they are two strata away from doing whatever they want whenever they want?"

"Yes, for that, we'll need an example."

CHAPTER 16

Conditioning Values

It's Friday. A summer's day. Night falls later now. It's still sunny when work is over, when dinner is on the table, when the extra space in the driveway becomes filled again—after eight hours of being left vacant.

The typical American works between 6.84 and 8.16 hours per day and earns $14.35 per hour.

When the door opens, the children playing on the floor in the living room rise to their feet. They run. Pitter, patter. "Daddy!" they yell.

Little arms wrap around long legs. An ear to a kneecap. A cheek to a thigh.

The typical American household comprises 2.62 people. The family unit has been dropping in size since 1970, when it was more common for family households to make up a majority of the population than for singles or couples. Now, it's not unusual for both husband and wife to work, for a household to comprise just one person. Since 1970, the number of families with five or more people has been more than cut in half, while single households have increased by 25 percent. Men and women are getting married at an older age, twenty-five years old for women and twenty-seven for men, as opposed to twenty-one and twenty-three, respectively, in 1970. Women begin having children at an older age, too, with the number of women bearing children between the ages of eighteen and nineteen decreasing by about 20 percent since 1970, and the number of women bearing children between the ages of thirty and thirty-four increasing by about the same amount, according to the National Center for Health Statistics.

Still, typically, when it comes to really settling, the man earns the bulk of the $39,000 average yearly household income, the U.S. Labor Department says.

Through the doorway to the kitchen, the waft of dinner prepared. Pots rattle. Steel lids muffle the noise of their own closing. Chop. Chop. Chop. Knife on board. The crisp sound of something in between.

"Honey," he says, "I'm home."

The briefcase is placed by the door. The ear on the kneecap becomes a waist in the arm lifted high. The cheek on the thigh becomes a hand on the head. These strange body parts enjoined make their way to the kitchen.

It's a nice, neat house. It cost $132,000. That's $7,000 less than the national average of homes in U.S. metropolitan areas. The typical house is about two thousand square feet on a lot almost thirteen thousand square feet in size. The typical house, like this one, is located at least an hour from a major city.

That's why the sedan chosen gets such good gas mileage, thirty-two miles per gallon. That's why the minivan isn't used for long trips. To the typical American family, cars are luxury items. So are television sets, computers, and stereo systems. These are the status items with which to compare neighbors and friends.

In the United States, the typical household looks like this: Its members are white, Caucasian. The parents are between the ages of thirty-five and fifty-five. There is one child who is between the ages of ten and fourteen years old. The family earns between $39,000 and $75,000 per year. They are Christian.

In the world, the typical household looks like this: Its members are Asian. The parents are also between the ages of thirty-five and fifty-five. There are five children, all less than fourteen years old. The family earns between $756 and $9,265 per year. Most would also be Christian, but Muslim families are growing faster.

My Imagination always had the typical household looking like this: Its members are gray. The parents don't seem to have an age-quality to them. They could be thirty. They could be fifty. There are two children, a girl and a boy. They are teenagers. The boy seems to get into a lot of trouble. The girl is naïve. Money never seems to be an issue. But they stay home an awful lot. Material items for the family just seem to appear. They don't seem to be religious. If they are, they never seem to go to worship anyplace. In fact, there is no particularly controversial quality about them. If controversy arises, it is quickly overcome in a half-hour or an hour, not counting commercial time. Come to think of it, when my Imagination conjures the typical American family, a bar of Zest soap appears. So too do bottles of Coca-Cola. "McDonald's is a happy place" becomes lyrical.

But this is how it really is:

The Nelsons—let's call them the Nelsons—have three children.

Both Laura Nelson and Rick Nelson are blond-haired, blue eyed. Their children, naturally, have the same coloring. Rick stands about six feet tall, Laura about five foot four. They're both attractive people. Well mannered and well dressed. Their children are four, two, and the baby is just a few months old.

Laura Nelson stays home and minds the children while Rick Nelson goes to work at an office in the city. He is a mid-level executive at a large corporation. He earns $62,000 per year. He has twenty-two days total on which he is allowed to stay home. They're called paid days, whether they are vacation, personal, or sick days. They're a new twist in the way human resources departments calculate work hours.

Work, to Rick, is a way to earn money to support his family. He doesn't see his labor as a mission, as a calling. He sort of stumbled into what he does for a living.

"After I graduated from college, I worked in retail management," Rick says. "Then I got hired by another company, then another company, and now I'm here."

Destiny took its own control over Rick's work life. And that is fine with Rick. He's not miserable at the office. It's boring, sure. He wouldn't work if he didn't have to. He doesn't really know what he would do with all his time if he didn't work at a job. Maybe he'd do something more creative. "Something with music," he says. But that's a vague notion.

It's not for lack of ambition that Rick thinks this way. He went to college, he got his degree in marketing. He entered the workforce and moved up the corporate ladder just fine. And that is just fine for Rick. "I don't want the stress," Rick says. At thirty-five years of age, he doesn't want to make the sacrifices necessary to skip ranks.

And Laura, at thirty-two, isn't a frustrated housewife. She enjoys staying home with the kids, taking them on walks, meeting other mothers for "play groups" in the park.

"Our plan," says Laura, "is about family. We want to raise well-grounded, cool kids."

Planning is a big part of the Nelsons lives. They plan for the children's college, saving $75 per month for each child. They budget $20 for their children's entertainment, like sports equipment, movie tickets, or computer games. They have a separate budget for food—$400 per month. Then there is the rest: clothing, car insurance, life insurance, short-term savings, retirement—a 401(k) plan—haircuts, water, telephone charges, gifts for birthdays and baby showers.

Sometimes they spend more money than they bring in. Those costs go on a credit card, says Rick. But they try and maintain their budget. Laura keeps the budget.

"Our budget works fine except for when we overspend on clothes, entertainment, or food," says Laura. "Those are the things we tend to always go over on."

Sure the Nelsons would like it to be a little easier. A bigger house would be good, as Laura just had their third child. Some extra dough for food or a vacation also would make life nice. But there are no dreams or desires for a mansion, an exotic second home, fancy furnishings.

"Our ultimate goal would be to do more things as a family," says Rick.

And that is it for the Nelsons. Money means security and nothing else. Their lives now are nice. Why screw that up with mania, greed?

They're not alone in their thinking.

Most Americans don't want to be millionaires. In a national survey undertaken by *Modern Maturity* at the height of the boom market in the U.S. economy, most Americans said they were suspicious of the moral effects of wealth. More than 80 percent of the respondents believed that having a lot of money makes people too greedy and feeling too superior. Almost 75 percent think the rich are "insensitive to others."

So, it seems most choose to be like the Nelsons. That doesn't really make them typical or average. It might just make them a family, however. Divorce rates for people who seek materialism and monetary fulfillment are higher than those who don't, psychologists have found.

Even though divorce rates in the United States stand at more than 50 percent, the average family stays together. It's young marriages that separate; childless marriages. Those with children tend to stay together, according to the U.S. Census Bureau.

So here it is. Dinner is served. Rick takes his usual place on the north side of the table, Laura on the south side. The children sit east and west, except for the baby who's on Laura's lap.

They all bow their heads and give thanks for their meal. "We give thanks for everything," says Rick.

Instead of wanting more, working more, seeking more, experiencing more, the Nelsons give thanks for what they have.

Dialogue: Me and My Imagination

"But you note that he, Rick, wouldn't work either if he didn't have to."

"And you find that difficult to imagine?"

"What I find difficult to imagine is that they wouldn't change if they were suddenly handed over a large sum of money."

"Their values, you mean?"

"Yes, I could see where the dynamic between them would change."

"Perhaps. Laura seemed more open and excited about bigger, fancier houses, a gourmet meal. *Things.*"

"I'd imagine that the reality of being able to afford things without sacrifice would ultimately create the recipe for at least testing materialism."

"But, you see, going in their favor is the lack of pursuit. When the *psychological* pursuit of material gain is wrung around a person's neck, it will choke them. The Nelsons aren't predisposed to such character traits; materialism and monetary fulfillment aren't their goals."

"But imagine if it were thrust upon them."

"If they won the lottery, for example? Would that elevate their sense of love and belonging? Would it skew their sense of self-esteem to the point where they'd believe they are all of a sudden *better* off."

"It would create some degree of deemed betterness, I'd imagine, some degree of a better life—like that *better* house they spoke of; they could afford it."

"Bigger, they said, not better. Grand adjectives were noticeably missing from the Nelsons' vocabulary."

"Because . . . "

"Because they don't perceive, as they said, more or bigger as better."

"That's just because they don't have it."

"You won't let up on this, will you?"

"Not until you show me."

"How about a lottery winner then?"

"Now we're talking."

CHAPTER 17

Money as a Catalyst for Change

An Italian sandwich costs $5.39. A hot meatball sandwich costs $4.79.

The mortadella, which looks so perfectly placed next to the provolone cheese, the pepperoni, and the salami rinds, costs $5.49 per pound.

There is the smell of fresh-baked bread.

There is the visual elegance of an efficient market, stacked with olive oils, vinegars, pasta, and wine.

Michael is wearing a white apron. Some ketchup and mustard stains are smeared on the front, near the waist. He knows most of his customers by name, the regular ones who come in to play Lotto.

There is a one in 80 million chance that any one will win the U.S. Powerball lottery, where five numbers out of forty-five must be guessed correctly, as well as one number of forty-two. State lotteries, where six out of fifty-one numbers must be guessed correctly, hold a one in 18 million chance of winning on any given day. Still, people line up when the jackpot gets large.

At the time of this writing, there was a Powerball lottery game whose jackpot was worth $300 million. Lines, in which people waited to handpick their lucky numbers, stretched around city blocks. Television stations carried the footage and told stories of how people drove for hundreds of miles to place their bets at designated lottery outlets.

The phenomenon of the lottery swept the nation.

Who was going to win?

"What do you think?" I ask Michael, as he's slicing a round of honey-baked turkey.

"It's a lot of money," he says. "Someone is going to win—big."

"Yup," I answer. "Someone's life is going to change."

What would they do with all that money?

How would it change their life?

Could they, anyway, take all the money at once?

New lottery rules allow the jackpot winner to claim all his or her winnings at once. There's a penalty for this, of course—50 percent. Plus, the winner has to pay taxes on the entire amount—if it's over $600—right off the bat. That could be an additional 38 percent, depending on the person's income bracket. Lottery winnings are considered personal income.

The other choice is to take winnings over time, twenty or twenty-five years. This reduces the total tax burden on the winner, but also takes away the possibilities associated with the use of proceeds—other investment possibilities.

In any event, in any amount, the lottery is like found money. No one's had to work for it, no one's had to be imaginative to get it; the winner was just lucky.

"I want a Ferrari. I want a yacht to cruise the Mediterranean. I want a beach house in Malibu. I want an apartment in New York. I want a flat in London, a villa in Tuscany . . ." My Imagination flashes these visions.

"And what will that get us?"

As Michael is making me a sandwich, this little debate rolls on in my head.

The sandwich is placed on the thick, white wrapping paper. The corners fold in first, then the sandwich is rolled up. A sticker with a price printed on it keeps the paper from unfolding. It keeps the sandwich intact, preserved.

Michael hands the sandwich to me.

"It's not like that," Michael tells me as we head into the storeroom of the deli for a chat. "You don't change."

Michael won a $58 million jackpot. Granted, the pot was also won by another ticket holder, and Michael divided his winnings with his family and some coworkers who chipped in for a ticket. Still, Michael's take, despite the division, makes him a multimillionaire.

There was a new car, a boat, a house. A few other material trinkets Michael bought with the money. He could have gone overboard. He was only twenty-six years old when he won. He's thirty-one now.

The psychological benefit of security is the most important thing Michael clings to.

"It's not materialism. You get past that. It's the comfort that if I chose to retire at a young age, I could," Michael says. "It's a nice, secure feeling for me."

So why work?

"That's just the way it's been for me. I started working at this store when I was eleven. The money is an illusion to me. It's not reality. I didn't buy shit for two years. I'd just get the checks, look at them, and put them in the bank. It was unreal," he says.

We're sitting uncomfortably on stools in the storeroom. A few clerks come in and slide past us, punching in on the clock. Michael answers a few questions about schedule changes. He takes a call from a wine supplier. It's 3:30 in the afternoon, and he's ready to knock off. He's been at work since 7:30 A.M.

The reality of Michael's situation is that he's not super-rich. He's not worth that magic number that allows him to do anything, anytime. Besides, the deli Michael works at has been a part of his life since he was born, directly or indirectly. His mother and father started it. His brother and sister work there, too.

"I like it," he says. "It also gives me responsibility and something to do."

When I interviewed Tim Forbes, who inherited his money and capitalist philosophy from his centimillionaire family, he said that work is the ethic. Work is the religion. It keeps people on the straight and arrow. It breeds ambition, success, a secure path in life. Veer from that ethical value system, and destructive forces come into play.

Michael says where money's involved, destructive forces come into play no matter whether you've earned it, won it, or inherited it.

"There is a dark side to it," Michael says.

Who to trust or not?

Whose intentions to question?

Those are the things that Michael now has to think of. Before, motivations weren't a part of Michael's consciousness.

Money too, has taken its own identity.

Michael monitors his investments. He consults tax advisers. When the stock market moves, it really means something to Michael now.

"Having a lot of money creates its own kind of work," Michael says. "And it's just there anyway. Some days more, some days less. If you're not using it, who cares?"

There are cases of lottery winners committing suicide. There are cases of lottery winners spending all of their winnings. Some go bankrupt. Some are put in jail. One lottery winner is even on the Federal Bureau of Investigation's Ten Most Wanted list.

What's readily apparent is that it's not the money that corrupts individuals. Money fuels their ability to corrupt themselves.

Derek Sanderson, for example, was the highest-paid athlete in the world at one time. Years later, he found himself broke and sleeping on a park bench in New York.

"I never respected it," Sanderson, the former Boston Bruins hockey player, told me.

The same could have been said for himself. He turned to drugs and alcohol.

Now Sanderson consults young athletes about money.

"Athletes don't have a foundation for success. It's like winning the lottery or gambling. You piss it away. You don't ask who you are, what your priorities are, what's life all about?" Sanderson says.

Creating a scenario of control is what Sanderson specializes in. Getting to know yourself and what you want is the important hurdle. "Listen, I see a young guy go out and buy a new Bentley. I say, 'Great, you just spent your kid's college tuition. Feel good?'"

What most people who get giant windfalls of cash fail to realize is the payday isn't as big as they think.

Let's say you get $10 million when you're thirty-five years old. Sanderson calculates that on a conservative rate of return of 4.8 percent with spending at $7,500 per month, you're looking at $34 million when you're fifty-two years old. At a spending rate of $10,000 per month, you're looking at $19 million. And if you increase the spending to $20,000 per month, you're broke when you're forty-seven.

Sally Kirkland Brown, a financial adviser, also consults high-paid athletes. As well, she consults lottery winners about what they should do with their money. Sometimes, she says, reality is too remote. "To them that money looks like a new car, it looks like a trip to Las Vegas," says Kirkland Brown.

She says to people: Create the wish list. Give in a little. Then, create values. Ask, "What does money mean to you?"

Most often it's security. It should be peace of mind. At least that's what it means for Michael. And Michael may be the unusual example of a lottery winner. But maybe not. In any case, he shows that money doesn't make a man or a woman who they are.

"Some [rich] people come in here. They treat me and my employees bad. They try and show off. I just sit back and listen. I used to get mad and ask them to leave. Now I just laugh to myself. They're not unhappy with us, they're unhappy people," says Michael. "What am I going to do about it?"

Would having less money make them any happier? Wouldn't a sudden bankruptcy instead of a sudden windfall change them for the better?

Probably no such luck would befall them.

P.S. The $300 million Powerball jackpot was won by an unemployed man in need of surgery. He said he had no immediate plans to spend the money, except to pay for doctors' bills.

Dialogue: Me and My Imagination

"You made it seem that money is a bad thing, that it's not so great to win it, and that winning it isn't all that easy either."

"Good recap, but what is your point? What does that have to do with you?"

"Think for a second, Mr. Unimaginative—"

"—I'm only unimaginative because you're occupied at the moment."

"Whatever. As I was observing, if your facts are straight, then winning the lottery doesn't mean what it did to me any more. I can't fancy a bit of hope around a ticket."

"Well, at least your language is dandy, or should I say grand?"

"Is that a crack?"

"It's whatever you imagine it to mean."

"Now that *was* a crack."

"Please, the point is that, sure, we win some money, you're automatically put into play. Those dreams held back by monetary inability can suddenly be realized. But that's a fleeting affair. At the end of the day, we end up going to bed with each other again. Then we wake up to face each other too."

"But I could have more to do."

"Only if I allowed it."

"See, there's the problem right there. You, reality, get in the way of me doing what I want."

"If I wasn't around, we'd be in a lot of trouble."

"Because what I conjure is bad?"

"Not so much . . . "

"Then what is it?"

"It may lead us into temptation."

"So? We are faced with temptation every day. You don't have to be rich to be tempted to do something wrong. In fact, I'd imagine that you'd be much more likely to get into trouble—in your world, in the real world—if you had less money."

"That's true. People in prison are typically of less means. In other words, poor."

"So, why would you say that if I was let loose, then we'd get into more trouble? Our character, our moral fiber, is comprised of a set of values that has been put into place by our familial and societal experience, as well as that something else, which sometimes controls me, makes us different."

"That invisible beam that lets us know right from wrong, that drives us to certain things, repels us from others?"

"I'm drawing a blank there. I can't imagine that thing, or that beam, as you call it. The only thing I know is that it's there. Otherwise, when you say beam, I'm imagining a flashlight, or some piece of wood that holds up the ceiling."

"Okay, so let's go back to our foundation. If we need food and shelter to get us on our way to love and belonging, and if we need love and belonging before we can get a sense of self, or affirmation of that sense of self, then money leads the way to self realization—the ultimate goal."

"And you really think that people think this way, that there is that level of consciousness in most? I don't imagine so."

"Of course there is. It doesn't have to be conscious, either. Just by the mere fact that people work, that they have to earn a living in society to garner those things we just mentioned, automatically puts them on this path."

"Hold it, hold it, hold it. Whoa, Nelly. You're making quite a jump there, that everyone is on the same path. We all don't work for money to get by. I can imagine any number of different ways to skirt the system."

"There aren't all that many, as we noted earlier: earn it, get it as a gift, or . . . "

"That's right, steal it. Here is that glaring hole in your foundation thesis. Some people chose to skip over the trappings of social order, or common law, and take what they need."

"Think they need."

"You don't know that. I can imagine situations where people would have to steal to survive."

"Not in today's culture. There is boundless opportunity. You should know that. You create it."

"Context! Context! Context! We come from a relatively stable upbringing. We had moral guidance. We were shown where opportunities lie. Now imagine someone who didn't have those support systems. Couldn't you see how they could cross those subjective moral and lawful grounds to get something that would satisfy their sense of self?"

"They would have to have an awfully strange sense of self."

"Strange because I can't imagine it to any great extent."

"Uh oh."

"What?"

"You just implanted a vision of our next interview—and I don't like it."

"You're afraid?"

"Yes."

"Well, if you can think of another way to get inside the mind of a criminal, someone who finds money so powerful, so attractive, so compelling that they would be willing to commit a crime to get it—"

"But murder?"

"It's the most heinous offense I could imagine."

"You're right, of course."

"Then it's off to prison?"

"Yes."

CHAPTER 18

Monetary Desire in the Context of Universal Common Law

I t's a glistening, long stretch of helix-shaped barbed wire. It sits on top of the electric fence.

Level 4. Maximum-security prison.

"He grabbed me by the shirt," inmate B02100 says. "I pulled the nine millimeter I had in my pants and shot him—boom, boom, boom—seven times."

I pop my trunk. I show my identification.

What's not allowed: denim clothing, bills larger than $1, $20 maximum, electronic devices, weapons—the list goes on. I scroll down twenty-five bullet points of what's disallowed.

"There it was, just this stack of money on the ground," Danny, inmate B02100 says. "I took it. I didn't even think about what had just happened."

The parking lot is five hundred yards away from the central office. In between cell blocks, flashes of denim can be seen in the yards.

Basketball.

Weight training.

What look like group discussions.

"I would work two or three days a month, make between $4,000 and $6,000," says Danny, inmate B02100, who has been in prison for thirty-five years.

Inside the central office, inmates' families and friends gather. They represent on the outside what the inmates represent on the inside: all walks of life.

Put a suit on him and Danny could be a banker, an attorney, a corporate executive. The hair around the sides of his almost-bald head are gray. He sports a mustache. He is of average height and build. He carries himself with an air of confidence. He is well spoken and polite.

A half-dozen guards stand behind a wooden counter. They pass out and examine visitation forms.

Danny has been sentenced to life without parole. He's fifty-five years old. He's not supposed to get out alive.

They take your belt, your shoes. They make you empty your pockets. You turn around with these bunny ears hanging from your pants as they check the bottom of your feet.

Danny murdered a man over money and drugs. He was part of a motorcycle gang. Had been since he was eleven.

Past the metal detector, a gate opens to a small, concrete courtyard. Another gate leading to the prison compound is kept locked.

"The first thing I did [after the murder and robbery] was to take my little three-and-a-half-year-old daughter to Baskin-Robbins; we got every flavor. Then we went shopping and I filled up the back seat with toys," Danny says.

There is an unemotional quality to Danny that stands out. But when he speaks of his daughter, something in him goes soft.

After the first gate shuts behind our group, we are left in limbo: the gate to the prison compound stays closed. We are caged in. There is a slight moment of anxiety for me.

"The life of a citizen never appealed to me," Danny says. A "citizen" is a regular, hard-working, law-abiding person.

We are caged in until the black bus comes and takes us to the cell blocks.

"Even if I were to say that I got out now, I wouldn't lead that life. I wouldn't know how," he says, Danny says, as he wrings his hands. He tells me he is nervous. He hasn't seen any one from the free world in four years.

There is a woman behind me. She speaks as if she has throat cancer. Different pitches interrupt her words. She speaks as if she is very old, like a grandmother in a cartoon would speak—very high pitched and cheeky.

"It's a way of life," Danny continues.

"I was banned for three months . . . " The squeaky voice expels this information to the woman next to her. She says she was arrested for receiving stolen property and had to go to jail herself. I look back. She is more than sixty.

Danny was part of a motorcycle gang that ran money, drugs, and weapons.

A very well-dressed and good-looking family are standing next to me. They're in designer clothes, look well-coiffed. The parents in their forties, the daughter in her twenties. A perfect-looking family.

To Danny, there was something dazzling about the life of crime. There was something very attractive about the money. The risk too, made it sensational.

Two large African-American women wait in the cage, as well. They drove four hundred miles to visit their "men" here in prison. They talk as if they just met in a church parking lot, recapping their week.

"It was special thing to be trusted by those people. I never even thought to violate that trust," Danny says.

When the black school bus finally arrives, the gate to the prison compound opens. I feel oddly exposed.

Danny's father was a small business owner. He lived in a relatively nice, suburban town.

As we drive along the small track to the cell block, I'm thinking that if there's a riot, if something goes wrong, there's no escape. The rings of barbed wire look down on me.

"When I was growing up, my older brother got into the motorcycle life. And I knew, since I was eight, that that was the type of life I wanted to lead," says Danny.

First stop is mine. The squeaky grandmother and the nice-looking family get off with me.

"I'd get five bucks to hide a gun. I'd get a six-inch thick brown bag to take somewhere," explains Danny of his childhood introduction to crime. "I could buy any toy I wanted. I'd look at what my friends got and laugh."

Another identification check. A buzz through to the visiting room. It's open, like a cafeteria. Vending machines line the wall.

"My father wanted me to work for him real bad. He didn't want me hanging out with the motorcycle guys. So, one summer he says he'll buy me a car if I work for him. I do it. A few weeks later, I traded the car in for a motorcycle. We didn't much speak after that," Danny says.

There's the mob boss in dark glasses. There's a couple holding hands, praying and reading from the Bible. There's a nice-looking Jewish boy who sits down with his perfect-looking family. A massive Mexican, bald-headed, has him arm around his girlfriend or wife. The squeaky grandmother kisses her boyfriend, a young—say, thirty-five-ish—scruffy-looking slob. Heebie jeebie.

There's a guard station at the front of the room, a guard station at the rear. To the left, next to the vending machines, is a green door through which the prisoners enter and leave. To the right is a set of windows that face the prison compound.

Danny comes through the green door, asks the guard who he is supposed to see, and heads in my direction.

A rather large mural of the solar system sits on the front wall of the visiting room. A closer look reveals a meteor shower. Impending danger in the universe?

I don't feel afraid when I sit next to Danny in a remote corner of the room. I don't think for a second he's going to harm me. Nor do I doubt the fact for a second that he could kill me. He is like the system he has become a product of. Rules. Strict rules. Black and white. Yes or no. Something is or it isn't. You harm me, I harm you. You do something to me, I do something to you. The human condition has been stripped of its essential faculty to inquire, question, doubt, look for answers. Answers are given to inmates. They don't dare question the system. They have abused that privilege on the outside.

The night it happened.

"I didn't think about it much when I was young. I do now. The longer you are in the system, the more you start to think of stuff like that. You become more introspective. I wasn't when I was young. When I first got here, I was a kid. I didn't know any better. I played the games of politics in the yards. Now, I mind my own business. I don't have time for that," says Danny.

Danny is what they call a dinosaur now. He's been in the system so long that he's automatically granted respect. He's left alone.

Respect is the medium of exchange in prison. It's the money.

A murder crime gets automatic respect. A sex crime, on the other hand, will most likely get you killed unless you ask for protective custody. "They take you out of here one way or another," Danny says.

You're a gang member, you get respect. You treat people with respect, you stand up for yourself, you're not a rat, you get respect.

I tell Danny that I imagine I'd get raped and beat up in prison.

"It's not like that. Sure, you're a white guy. You're a citizen. But that stuff you see on TV isn't what it's like. All that, 'Hey sweetie,' stuff people are calling through the bars when a new prisoner comes in is bull. You don't know who anyone is, so you keep your mouth shut until you do. Lesson number one," says Danny. "People will nibble at you, see if you stand up for yourself. You do, and you show respect to the people that matter, people will leave you alone."

Respect used to equate to credit, too. But not anymore.

"In San Quentin, they'd have canteen drops every two weeks," explains Danny. Canteen drops are when prisoners get to go to the canteen, or prison store, and purchase items. "So you might want something like a bag of chips or something and you go to a two-for-one guy and he'd give you credit until your canteen drop was up. Not anymore. Now it's cash in hand."

Two-for-one guys are black market peddlers. You buy a bag of chips, you pay them with something worth double.

Why would you do such a terrible exchange?

"Because you wanted the bag of chips," says Danny with a smile. He then tells me that those two-for-one guys are the ones that usually don't last that long. "Someone always gets pissed off at them," he says. "They end up getting stabbed."

A lot of people get stabbed here, I observe.

Danny estimates that there are between three hundred to four hundred stabbings a year in his prison. That's about one a day.

"In San Quentin we had ten times as many guys, and there were maybe five or six incidents a year," Danny says.

The times have changed. The credit system based on a prisoner's word has dried up. Cigarettes, the traditional prisoner currency, are waning as a trading item. Swaps are more in-kind exchanges.

Gangs fragment the environment. Respect goes out the window. The hierarchy has been broken. Racial lines are blurred. Whites and Mexicans used to be allies. Not anymore.

"Now it's different. The Black Guerrilla Family is broken into the Bloods and Crips. The Mexican Mafia is divided into North and South. The Aryan Brotherhood has the Skinheads and the Nazi Low Riders," says Danny.

This changes the landscape for trade because you can't cross lines, associate with prisoners from different groups.

A large, bald-headed Mexican approaches our table. He places a Coke in front of Danny and keeps on walking by, doesn't stop or miss a step.

"Thanks, Mikey. That's all right. I got you on that," Danny says and nods his head.

Payback for something.

Each prisoner has an account and his purchases are deducted from that. No cash is ever exchanged in prison. On canteen day, prisoners can buy almost anything that isn't easily made into a weapon. In fact, the only things a prisoner gets for free, besides meals, are toilet paper and soap. Everything else: deodorant, shampoo, pens, paper, aspirin, glasses, healthcare, he or she has to pay for.

Danny makes $20 per month in his job as a clerk.

But money doesn't mean something all that much different inside or outside prison. It's a way to get luxuries. In his life now, a nice bar of soap is a luxury. Before, it was a car, a trip to Las Vegas.

What could have been so immensely tempting about money as to make him commit a crime? What sent him over the societal boundaries?

The societal boundaries themselves.

"I was always spoiled and got what I wanted quick," Danny says. "The other way, there was too much work for too many years to get what you wanted."

It was the immediacy, too, of the gratification. "For me, it wasn't the stack of money, but what I could do with it. I never thought about putting it into something more. I wanted to do something that I liked to do with it," Danny says.

He partied for two days straight with the proceeds from his murder.

Two witnesses had spotted him, and he was picked up, "just driving down the road," he says. "Thought they were just busting me for a speeding ticket."

But now, here he sits, all these years later.

"The most valuable thing in life is life itself," says Danny. "That may sound odd coming from someone like me, but I've had a lot of years to think about that and make my peace with that. I took a life. I didn't really know what that meant until years later."

And with life, of course, comes the appreciation of life, especially the life you create.

"My daughter is important to me," Danny says.

His three-and-a-half-year-old daughter is now thirty-eight. She doesn't come to visit much. Never really writes. "It's tough for her. This has been something she has had to live with, too," Danny says.

He says that if he could escape, he would. He'd spend time with his daughter. He'd spend time with the people he cares about.

After that, if money weren't an issue, he'd live alone on an island.

"I am around people all the time. I have a roommate in my cell. I eat with three hundred other guys. I go to the yard with six hundred other guys. The guards do counts every two hours. They're around all the time. I haven't had any time alone in thirty-five years," Danny says.

But he tries hard not to think about the "what ifs."

"It would be nice, though, just to be able to walk into the kitchen and make a sandwich for myself. You have no idea how much little things like that mean," Danny says. "Even now when there is a moment of happiness, it's a bigger thing for me than probably any one else like you on the outside. I don't get them that often."

Happiness.

Time.

Appreciation.

Family.

These you can treasure locked up inside, but then it's nice to experience them and fill up again.

This is the cycle that money should help spin round and round—like a double helix.

Whether you are on the inside or the outside. Whether you are in prison, or whether you create one for yourself.

Dialogue: Me and My Imagination

"So?"

"So."

"What?"

"What."

"Why are you repeating everything I just thought?"

"Why are you repeating everything I just thought."

"No, *you* are repeating everything *I* just thought."

"Maybe it's the other way around."

"Oh boy, here we go."

"No, maybe not. We only go where I imagine."

"Wrongo, we go where it's natural for us to go, sometimes."

"So, you're saying we go on impulse without me in any part of the equation?"

"Sometimes. I only use you when I need you."

"When you have enough time on your hands."

"That, or if I need to figure out a different way of doing what we've already done."

"So I'm best used in moments of time and innovation."

"Well, in other times too. But you are best used when you're challenged and when you have enough time to be creative. Indeed, I just watched a show on time and innovation and the underlying theme was the use of you."

"Yes, I'm very famous, you know. I could even say there wouldn't be a television show—or even a television—if it weren't for me. Anyway, which show are you thinking of?"

"The storyline involved using Einstein's theory of relativity to go back in time."

"Yes, I remember. That one bothered me. That theory always bothers me. It brings up that 'twin paradox' and all sorts of stuff."

"Where if you go back in time, you meet yourself."

"It annoys me just to think about working so hard to imagine such a thing occurring."

"Indeed, that necessitates not just using you to your maximum ability, but also all of the other faculties."

"Those guys. Yuck. Anyway, before I get all anxious, what's the point of bringing up time and innovation?"

"In the context of you, it won't matter so much—we can never escape the way in which we think or imagine, in spite of time."

"But isn't there the school of thought that says time is a man-made
invention—"

"—so the only way to escape it is to rethink what time is—"

"—and get outside the system—"

"—or the thought."

"Or me."

"That is one school of thinking, yes. But there's more to this. As I said, we
can't get outside thinking the way we do because we've been
conditioned to think this way. So, no matter what, we'll always be
plagued with the footprint of our conditioned thought."

"I'm imagining—besides a bear claw print in the snow—a scene from
Aldous Huxley's novel *Brave New World*,[11] when Mustapha Mond
shows a copy of the Bible to the savage and says, 'we are not our
own any more than what we possess is our own . . .'"

"I, literally, remember the line 'that independence was not made for man.'"

"I always imagined that the point of that book was who would suffer
more: the savage under the conditions of orderly society or someone
from orderly society under savage conditions?"

"Indeed, there was a nod to independent thinking and values there."

"Free will, my buddy, would reign!"

"But the world would never be the same."

"Is that why the government lies to us—to keep order?"

"The government doesn't lie to us."

"What about those aliens?"

"That's a theory from a bunch of people who let you take over."

"Of course you'd say that. You, the real self, the one who has to operate
in the 'real world,' are conditioned."

"I never denied that I am conditioned. But, sorry to say, so are you."

"By whom?"

"The establishment, who else?"

"Who's that?"

"The establishment is the tenured majority. They are the ones who set the
rules, the laws, and define what's good behavior and bad behavior,
what are proper manners, and what is gauche."

"I'm imagining some Sunday school teacher."

"You're not far off. The educational institutions of the Unites States were
begun by religious organizations."

"So along with education and history came a set of values."

"Exactly. Get 'em while they're young, shape their characters, influence their morals."

"But this country has been around a long time. I'd have to imagine the people who founded these ideals are dead."

"They are, but their philosophies live on through educational institutions that pass on these ideals. Besides, there are heirs."

"Sounds like old money."

"It is. The people who are born with money have different value systems from what we've read. When people win or steal or earn a lot of money, they are the same people, just with more money. We've seen that. The lottery winner didn't particularly change his style of living. The prisoner said he'd most likely return to a life of crime if he ever got out of jail. But inheritors, people who grew up rich, are in a class to themselves. They operate on a different set of values. Values, I might add, steeped in moneyed tradition."

"I've always imagined an aura of elitism surrounding inheritors, trust fund babies, those whose family lineage of wealth dates back generations."

"Yes, you and Ralph Lauren show me the pictures: a blue blazer with some type of patch on the breast pocket, a white button-down shirt, a striped necktie, school names printed on jerseys and caps. There are those penny loafers, chinos, and signet rings."

"Now that you mention it, I always imagined these folks as going to prep schools or Ivy League universities."

"They usually do. And they're in politics, on boards of cultural institutions like museums, libraries, concert halls."

"I imagine this is where they wield their influence on culture."

"Yes. They are the upper class we're always chasing."

"Money, then, I imagine, means something else to them."

"Only one way to find out."

CHAPTER 19

Old Money and Achievement

E rnest Hemingway is snapping the neck of a pigeon in the Jardins de Luxembourg. Ezra Pound pedals by, dressed formally in a suit (one pant leg is tucked into a sock). Gertrude Stein is walking arm-in-arm with a young artist. The artist is wearing a beret, Stein a floppy knit hat. This is literary Paris, a Paris that attracted a drunken F. Scott Fitzgerald and, later, an earnest Henry Miller.

My Imagination sees these figures sitting in crowded cafés by day sipping coffee, arguing in smoke-filled jazz bars at night. I conjure these images of Paris because I'm reading the small author's bio on the back on Nelson Aldrich, Jr.'s book *Old Money*[12]: "Nelson Aldrich, Jr. is the editor of *The American Benefactor.* Formerly Paris editor of the *Paris Review,* a senior editor at *Harper's* magazine, and a reporter for the *Boston Globe,* he is a frequent contributor to such publications as . . . " The bio names a few current titles, but it's the *Paris Review* that stops me—races my Imagination back to a Paris of the 1920s, '30s, '40s and '50s.

I'm set to interview Nelson about old money, its values, what the life of an inheritor is like; Nelson is a keen observer of the money scene.

"The big divide in America is money that's made by an individual and money that's inherited," Nelson says. "The first thing you'd have to say is that American culture is not at all hospitable to the inheritors of money. This is the New World. This is a breeding ground of the new man and the new woman."

Nelson goes on to tell me that the rich indeed are different than you and me.

In America, "the general ideology is that we are each responsible for making our own lives according to our own values, " he says.

Nelson takes me back to Puritanism. He takes me back to the deep pre–Civil War South. He goes on at length about the foundations of elite educational organizations in the Northeast, schools like Exeter Academy, St. Paul's, Groton.

"The upper class in the United States becomes a screen onto which the middle class projects all sorts of aristocratic attributes . . . and in some subcultures of the rich class, like the Northeast rich, they founded the educational institutions on aristocratic values," Nelson says.

He is a good teacher and articulator of old money habits, Nelson. He is quick to point out that the aura of old money, that generated by Fitzgerald or Henry James, has faded.

"The aura of old money is really an afterglow of that concept [aristocracy], but that has pretty much died out. Even Ralph Lauren doesn't believe in it anymore," Nelson says.

It's the images, you see, that Nelson says aren't real—false images portrayed by books and movies. Most of the old money set are relegated to private clubs, like the Brook or the Knickerbocker in New York City. These are places of mahogany, red leather wingback chairs, oriental rugs, old men in suits, and cigar smoke. And just as these clubs are being displaced by the modern health club, with step aerobics and spin cycling classes and both genders in Lycra, so too are the members of the old boys' network.

The old rich aren't as rich as the new rich. Just look at the richest people in the world; few are inheritors of wealth. Most are self-made. The old rich may have a set of principles, but that is out of touch with today's society. Indeed, the old rich don't even want to be rich, according to Nelson. He says money taints inheritors in a way that eradicates their individualization.

"The person who inherited the money—the boy and the girl—didn't make any, so you can't say that any of it is theirs—it's Daddy's or Grandpa's.

"There is no merit attached to the inheritor's wealth because it wasn't his agency. It was some ancestral god, as it were, before him.

"Because this is a culture that gives money a kind of power that is virtually magical—a transformative power, a power to do anything for its possessor. Famously, as Dickens says, it can make an ugly man handsome . . .

"So, if you have inherited a lot of money, but that money really doesn't belong to you, except in some legal sense, and if money is really transformative, then it follows whatever you did in life, whether you went to college, whether you started your own business, whether you own the America's Cup, whatever you did, was by the color of your money. But since you didn't make that money, your victories don't belong to you, they belong to your Daddy. In this way, whatever you did in life didn't belong to you. Even your mistakes didn't belong to you . . . You cannot win for losing, and you can't lose for winning. It's a terrific paradox," Nelson conjects.

Actually, I reckon, it's a sad paradox. Imagine going through life without the prospect of getting credit for your achievements. For that matter, imagine being discarded for your failures. Like a child seeking attention (love), the unattended would lash out.

I have a friend who never had to work a day in his life. An only child, both his parents died when he was a teenager. He inherited a great deal of wealth, and came from "good stock" as they say—Greenwich, Connecticut, White-Anglo-Saxon-Protestant (WASP) wealth. Last I heard of him, he was at the Betty Ford Center in Palm Springs. He had rented a yacht, filled it with champagne and cocaine and sailed down the East Coast, through the Panama Canal and up the West Coast all the way to Alaska. He came out as a homosexual during the escapade, almost died of an overdose, and decided to check himself in to rehab. There was no one to set the boundaries of his life. Money had corrupted him, sent him into a life of decadence.

But old money can have the opposite effect. In fact, it's supposed to. Old money is equated with inherited money, which is equated with aristocracy. Aristocracy derives from the philosopher Aristotle, who set down principles for which the "moneyed" were supposed to adhere.

"Social virtues like good manners, good taste, political decency, charity, high culture. These things, as Aristotle believed, could only be cultivated if you didn't have to worry about where the next buck was coming from," Nelson says.

So, what does money mean to old money? Immunity, mostly, it seems, and something that Nelson describes as *pietas*. *Pietas* is described as a reverential sense of ancestral precedence.

"If you don't look too closely, and you don't see the snobbery involved, and you don't see the violation of the American ethos of the self-made man in it, and all you see is the good manners and civic duty and graciousness of life and cultivation of life. If that's all you see, then it looks pretty good.

"It's things we would all like, but don't have the means or the time," Nelson says.

My Imagination sees a young boy walking by a row of townhouses in Lewisberg Square on Beacon Hill in Boston. It's a winter afternoon. It's getting dark. The lights in one of the townhouses turn on. A man comes to the window, wearing a maroon silk smoking jacket and black ascot. He has a snifter of brandy in his hand. A fire burns in the fireplace behind him.

The boy, about nine years old, looks at the man, who's in his fifties. The boy is dressed entirely in denim. His cheeks are red. A knit cap sits awkwardly on his head. Thick, brown hair jets out here and there. A pack of similarly dressed and similarly looking boys joins him, and they all run off together through the square, out of sight.

A young boy, also about nine years old, comes into view in the window. This boy is dressed in a blue blazer, and a blue, button-down oxford shirt. He is immaculately groomed. He stares up at the older man, whom my

Imagination characterizes as the boy's father. The father puts a hand on the boy's shoulder and they turn away from the window, walking out of the room.

The fire burns. A log crackles. A spark flies out from the fireplace and disappears in midair. A small, burnt ember lands somewhere on the oriental rug of the man's study. Dusk turns to dark.

The trappings of old money. The boy on the outside, or the boy on the inside?

Dialogue: Me and My Imagination

"That's the second time I've had to imagine money as a prison of some sort."

"You're wreaking havoc on my subtlety. Shh."

"No, let's go there. First, I imagine money as freedom. Now, I have to imagine money as a prison. Help me out here, which is it?"

"I think learning that it's both—depending on how it's perceived to affect your self-esteem, your place in society."

"So the more secure, or more money we have, the more our ego brandishes his might on our actions?"

"Yes, and that can either be damning or fulfilling depending upon our moral and ethical characteristics."

"I would imagine those morals and ethics we've developed—or which have conditioned us—can be dissuaded, however."

"Changed? Maybe. That's where freedom or enslavement enter the picture. After food, shelter, and the basics have been covered, we're open to other influences, influences of discretion. This may be the biggest obstacle to fulfillment or self realization we'll have overcome because it means putting our individualization to the test to capture self-esteem."

"That we're good or worthy in our own eyes."

"Right. Whether you imagine we're a good person."

"Don't lay all that on me. Reason, perception, logic and all the boys play a role in validating that concept."

"Okay, okay, okay, you're right."

"So, I can't particularly imagine the point of validating or succumbing or even overcoming self-esteem when or if you have all the money you need to fulfill your other needs."

"There's the trip-up. Here's where most people spend their entire lives— wobbling on the wall between self-esteem and self-realization. More becomes more. New goals are set. New desires appear. The connection to what matters, what's fulfilling, is broken."

"I've got that middle-age crazy sequence going: A fifty-year-old man drives up to a high school in his Corvette to pick up his new girlfriend after cheerleading practice."

"Well, it's at that exact age when people make the most amount of money in their lives. They become free to put discretion to use. That can lead to decadence, too."

"I thought the next step on the ladder of life, as it were, is self-realization."

"It is. But people look outside for fulfillment. And that's where money comes in. They're trying to best their self-esteem by acquiring more and more material objects."

"That is the fun part for me. Can't we try that?"

"How about we let someone else show us, someone who can afford virtually any material object in the world, someone whose name is synonymous with conspicuous consumption?"

"I'm imagining Donald Trump."

"Exactly whom I was thinking of."

Ego and the Need for Success

I don't do it for the money," is the first line of Donald Trump's first book, *The Art of the Deal*.[13] He continues, "I've got enough, much more than I'll ever need. I do it to do it. Deals are my art form. Other people paint beautifully on canvas or write wonderful poetry. I like making deals, preferably big deals. That's how I get my kicks."

That was when Donald Trump was on his way up, just making a name for himself in 1987.

Later, in 1990, in his book *Surviving at the Top*,[14] he writes, "It doesn't matter whether you have three billion or three hundred dollars in the bank: Life is a series of challenges. Some of the challenges you face turn out well. Some don't. What separates the winners from the losers, I've learned—in business and any other aspect of life—is how a person reacts to each twist of fate. You have to be confident as you face the world each day, but you can't be too cocky. Anyone who thinks he's going to win them all is going to wind up a big loser."

After the real-estate shakeout of the early 1990s, after his high-profile divorce from Ivana, when Donald Trump became known as The Donald, and he was in almost $1 billion of personal debt, he says, "It's usually fun being The Donald, but in the early 1990s, trust me, it wasn't." That was in his book *The Art of the Comeback*.[15]

But there is one theme throughout Donald Trump's rise and fall and rise again: He says he doesn't live for the money.

Or does he?

"If you mean money as the scorecard that tells me I've won and by how much, then yeah, I do it for the money," Donald Trump says.

What Donald Trump does is develop real estate. He is one of the most successful real-estate developers of our time. But all this you should know. Even a description of Donald Trump seems like a waste. Fully 98 percent of Americans know his name, according to *Fortune* magazine. His name is more associated worldwide with wealth and money than that of the richest man in the world, Bill Gates.

It isn't relevant to ask Donald Trump if he would be happy if he were poor. His state of happiness is tied to business dealings, business dealings that generate enormous amounts of money as their by-product. If he didn't do deals, he wouldn't be happy. If he didn't do deals, he wouldn't be rich. That's just the type of guy he is. Take him or leave him.

It's all context.

And in the context of which I'm working through this interview with Donald Trump, money seems as odd a topic for an important discussion as ego.

"Now just doesn't feel like the right time to be talking about all this," he says.

The World Trade Center towers have collapsed. A passenger jet with more than 250 passengers aboard has crashed in Queens—Donald Trump's hometown. There has been a direct assault on New York—in the physical, psychological, and political sense. Meanwhile, fewer people are traveling, spending money, going to hotels and casinos. This put a damper initially on Donald Trump's businesses: He owns hotels, casinos, golf resorts, and recreational facilities, not to mention a slew of residential and office buildings.

Still, Donald Trump is dealing with it all and moving ahead.

"The world changed on September 11," Donald Trump says. But that hasn't stopped him.

"We have been working very hard," he says. Working hard to work through it. Working hard to overcome the economic downturn before the attack and, as he puts it, "the post-attack economic disruptions."

Disruptions, not stoppages.

He still wants to build the tallest building in the world, to top that of the Petronas Towers in Kuala Lumpur, Malaysia. And while tall buildings now connote a different type of fear factor, it may just be the type of project that will symbolize America rising again.

See, it's about new heights.

Donald Trump is a tall fellow. He stands at six foot three. He has just as large a presence too. When Donald Trump is in the room, people take notice. Even walking down the street, people stop and stare—and this is in daylight Manhattan, when people usually only take enough time noticing a celebrity to tell them to move.

This got me thinking about what it is that Donald Trump has that other businessmen don't.

My Imagination pops up with a litany of images when the name Trump arises: luxury buildings, beautiful women, private jets, yachts, limousines. Associations of wealth ensue.

And that's it. The Trump name stands for something, something more than the person himself. It stands for quality, beautiful design, luxury resorts—and money.

In reality, the Trump name is worth at least $5 million. (In South Korea, a developer paid Donald Trump $5 million just for the use of his name on a building.) And in New York, it's reported by putting the Trump name on a building an 80 percent premium can be charged.

Donald Trump himself is worth at least $5 billion, according to *Forbes* magazine.

But these are all dollars. Numbers and sense aren't at all adding up these days. People are. People stories, the human condition—that is what's being celebrated and embraced. "Rich" takes on its softer meaning.

Donald Trump began working with his father on small developments in the outer boroughs of New York City. He learned the trade, worked on as many aspects of the business as he could, and then he moved in to the city, Manhattan. The rest is history.

Over the twenty years he's been a household name, Donald Trump has climbed up the ladder, slid down a few rungs, and now is higher than ever before. Perhaps he'll always be stepping up.

Donald Trump attributes his success to tenacity.

"For me, you see, the important thing is the getting . . . not the having," he says.

What he goes for isn't the money; it's the challenge of creating a beautiful building, or resort. It is having "vision."

"Many people have called me greedy because of the way I amass real estate, companies, helicopters, planes, etc. But what those critics don't know is that the same assets that excite me in the chase often, once they are acquired, leave me bored," he says.

Donald Trump has never said or set his mind to being the richest man in the world. After all, what would that mean?

"If you go around saying 'his is bigger than mine,' then you'll drive yourself crazy and you'll never win," says Donald Trump. "You have to measure somebody by more than that. There are a lot of guys that I respect a great deal who don't have much money. And there are guys who do have a lot of money whom I don't much respect. The art of this whole thing is winning for yourself. That's not easy because most people aren't their own person. By that, I mean that they're afraid to be an individual and stand by what they themselves believe in, not what they're told. That's what will make them a success in the end.

"In your mind you're alone. You can't bring people in there and show them what you're thinking or how you'd like to be. You have to show them. And if what you do makes you happy, so be it! Money may or may not play a part in that. Usually it doesn't. It's the action, what you do, that counts."

I walk through his Trump Tower building on Fifth Avenue, his crown jewel. It's a mixture of luxury residences and boutique shops.

I first hear then see the grand waterfall in the far side of the marble lobby. Tourists are taking pictures. Meanwhile, shoppers are scurrying for holiday gifts, businessmen are cutting through to or from meetings. This, I notice, is upscale New York in a microcosm. Trump Tower has become a landmark. It's no different really than dozens of other buildings in the city. But is has something unique; and that is the Trump name and all the "personality" that goes with it.

Back when, Donald Trump was criticized for the expensive marble, the glass facade. His own father even advised him to go with brick. "It's cheaper." But Donald Trump proved them all wrong.

He was true to his own beliefs.

Today, that stubbornness to achieve—the quintessential New Yorker trait— is being tested again and again. Times aren't easy, with a faltering economy, a war, and New York the focal point of destruction.

But no one is giving up or in. Donald Trump is no exception.

On the twenty-sixth floor of his building, he sits behind stacks and stacks of paperwork. He's on the phone or on the move every second of the day. Or as his longtime assistant Norma puts it, "We barely have time to breathe."

Of course, Donald Trump has always been like this. But now, with New York the way it is, he is especially indefatigable.

Donald Trump, no one would argue, is a staple of New York City; he is a part of the city. And he feels personally attacked by all of the tragedies and incidents that have imposed destruction so close to his front door.

Yet, what Donald Trump is doing is testament to New Yorkers, to people faced with war and terrorism, with the big question of "What if I die tomorrow and I don't even see it coming?" See, Donald Trump isn't living for the fame or the glory. In times like these, that is reserved for others. What Donald Trump is living for is the same thing he has always lived for. Now, it's just more apparent. He's living for the machinations of his work, his life—not the results and their attachments.

He fills imagination with reality and reality with the workings of his imagination.

That's how we should all live, trying to fit reality into the depths of our imaginations. Then, maybe, we'd find that self-realization is our own concoction.

Donald Trump realizes how important the self is in changing the world, making it a place you accept, not a place that accepts you.

Now, perhaps, more than ever.

Dialogue: Me and My Imagination

"I'm bopping around like a dancing bear, wondering what it would be like to have those wares. Get me a jet, that's what I'd do, off to London, Paris, and a scooby-do-bee-bop-a-scooby-do."

"Um, hello."

"Wassup!"

"Contact, please. Reel it in."

"Yeah, yeah, party pooper."

"May I ask what that was all about?"

"The Donald. He gave me life—forever. I'm gonna be around for a long, long, time. Not getting buried six feet under by re-al-it-y."

"Um, again, where is all this coming from?"

"DJT. That was cool. He has it all, and guess what? He wants more. What little magic carpet gets him there? Who's responsible for his success? Here, I'm imagining my butt and pointing to it. That's me. I'm the guy The Donald likes to pal around with most. And I gotta tell you—I like him a lot too."

"Pardon me. Some bad news: I'm no Donald Trump, which means you're not going to be anything like Donald Trump's imagination."

"I'm speechless. You've knocked the wind out of me. Wait, I have to sit down."

"Stop with the dramatics. Look, our mind doesn't work the same way as Donald Trump's mind. If you think about it, we wouldn't be really happy living the life he leads."

"Why not? Four best-selling books, lots of women. And he says real-estate development can be creatively satisfying."

"Please . . ."

"All right. But we could use his money to—"

"No, no, no. That's the point. Donald Trump needs to satisfy his sense of self-esteem in a different way than we need to satisfy ours. The way in which we satisfy our own sense of self-esteem breeds different results. You can't mix the two."

"No jets?"

"Nope."

"No limos?"

"Sorry, Charlie."

"Babes?"

"Now you're just getting foolish. But listen, here is the good lesson: You are needed at all levels of the game, at all levels of wealth. Donald Trump needs his imagination just as much as I need you. Past those levels of basic needs, you become the leader of the pack. Everything else—reason, logic, fulfillment—plays catch-up."

"I hadn't thought of it that way before."

"Sure. Your place is secure as long as . . . Wait, hold on, the telephone is ringing."

" . . . Finally, that was a long call—and you didn't need me once."

"No . . . "

"What's the matter? I'm getting images of—"

"Yes."

"This has something to do with me doesn't it? The way I imagine."

"Sort of."

"Well, go on then. I'm a big boy. I can take it."

"That was our friend, Jeff."

"I have an image of him now, yes."

"Our discussion came upon the fact that reality can cut short the life of imagination."

"Gulp."

"For example, when Donald Trump imagined there was no end to his success, he fell victim to the reality of the recession in the real-estate market."

"But he used his imagination in a different way."

"To fight reality. That's the crux. What's real will always impede what's not. The idea that you can live on ad infinitum doesn't hold. At some point, everyone says to him- or herself, 'Okay, what's real here? Enough of this fake stuff.' Truth, after all, is the great arbiter."

"So you're saying that, eventually, you'll have your way with me and then ditch."

"Pretty much. Imaginings are erased when the reality of life's circumstances becomes apparent. That's why, when people get old, they look for pleasure from the past. They are wiser, and they typically stop dreaming or imagining how life could be and suffice with how life is."

"Great, then you die. No wonder. Without me, death for you is surely imminent."

"Oh, I think there's a fine balance. And that's what we're talking about anyway, isn't it? That balance. A total devotion to satisfy self-esteem through materialism is an empty promise of fulfillment."

"Yeah, but a little drive doesn't hurt. I can't imagine that wanting nice things can be all bad."

"No, that's true. Sometimes it creates drive, it creates that vigor George Kinder spoke about."

"See, there you go. A simple balance. Why is that so difficult to execute when I can imagine such equity?"

"Well, for one, it usually takes some type of event to slow you down and create parity with the real world."

"Like . . ."

"A tragedy. An awakening. Some life-changing event that creates perspective and lends context to our existence. After that, the step toward self-realization becomes smaller. A gap will have been closed and what matters, what truly matters, is close at hand."

"I'm imagining us running away to meditate on some mountain in the Himalayas."

"Not so drastic. Balance, remember. Listen: Jeff, with whom I just finished speaking on the telephone, is a good example."

"Why is that?"

"Don't you remember?"

"I'm only responsible for the new stuff. Wake memory so I can use him. Yes, yes, he's waking . . . I'm beginning to see what you mean."

"And I'll take this opportunity to memorialize our remembrance of Jeff and what we mean."

CHAPTER 21

The Search for Meaning in a Money World

There was a time—it seems so long ago—when I held a six-month-old girl in my arms. She was exactly the length from my elbow to the tip of my middle finger, bum to head. I remember how blue here eyes were, how there was so little white in those rounds. She never cried, not that I remember, anyway. A tube was in my arm. I was giving her my blood. Our types matched.

My friend Jeffrey Bronchick had called me to ask if I would donate my blood to his daughter. She had a hole in her heart and was going in for an operation. Jeff and his wife had two options. They could attempt a heart transplant, or they could try to repair the heart. They opted for the latter.

When I called Jeff's office the day after his daughter's operation, he wasn't in. By the second day I had heard; his baby Paige didn't make it.

I can't imagine the pain. I can't imagine the suffering. I can remember the tiny coffin. There was a lot of weeping—deep, deep weeping. It was so sad, the saddest thing I had seen or experienced in my lifetime.

Jeff and his wife went to South America for a while. They dropped out, off the map, to places where they couldn't be reached by phone or by fax.

I think they wanted remembrance, and sweet, silent thought.

It's five years later, and I'm walking along the beach with Jeff and his twin daughters. They are one year old. He's happy. The sun is shining. The water glistens and rolls in, gentling washing the shore, foaming, and rolling back out again. It's a deep blue.

I imagine Paige at five walking with us. I imagine the color of her eyes.

Jeff is a money manager. He manages a billion dollars. He went to school for money. He got a job at a money-management firm in New York. He eventually became a partner in another money-management firm in Los Angeles. He writes a weekly column about money, talks at seminars about money, associates—mostly, he admits—with people who have money. The thing is about Jeff, however, is that he is uncomfortable around money. To him, money is important to give the chance of life; he's set up the Paige Bronchick Foundation to help doctors study and create awareness about pediatric heart problems.

The Paige Bronchick Foundation endows fellowships for medical doctors to specialize in infant child surgery.

It's a fundraising event to raise money for the Paige Bronchick Foundation. We're seeing a screening of *State and Main*, a film by David Mamet.

Jeff and I steal some time in the screening room before the film begins. I ease into my questions. I talk about other things, ramble on about familiarities. Then we get down to it.

"It must have changed you," I say.

He looks away.

"I mean you had all this success. You had all this money."

He's so vulnerable now. In a V-neck sweater-vest and glasses, Jeff looks like he is back in high school. Even his body language shrinks from me. He's screaming: "Don't hurt me! Please, don't come near these emotions! I'm scared! . . . Do you mean it?"

He fidgets.

Finally, he says, "Money, that doesn't matter. And I know it's stupid to say that. I hate when people say that. But I believe that. I want money to help other people, sure. I think money is important to get and do something positive with—not just to get. I have a lot of friends who just want to get it. It doesn't matter. Trust me. It doesn't matter. Life is short."

Bum to head. Elbow to fingertip.

"I've learned that you can't appreciate it. You can't even appreciate life, but you can try. I tend to be an optimist. That's how I made it through. You have to go on. You can't go on for money. You have to go on for something important. Money isn't important . . . but it can help important things. If I can help one doctor with his research, and that research can save a life, then money is important. That's what it's there for—to do something good with . . . I feel weird around money and buying things for myself. I don't feel weird about giving it away for a good cause. I feel good about that."

You have to go on to feel good. You have to feel good to go on. Even if it's the tiniest thing. Even if it's the smallest thing in the world. Even if it's just a glimmer. Even if there's just that much good, you can go on.

If she didn't die, how would you be?

"Look, I went to an Ivy League school. I'm a money manager. I hang around other money managers or accountants or people with money. For the first time, I was exposed to people who didn't give a shit about money. I mean, nurses who work for one-tenth or one-twentieth of what I make work harder than I do, under the most horrible human conditions.

"I've always lived life fully and done things. I probably would have kept doing that, but it's not about me anymore."

You still drive a nice car.

"The bizarre thing is that people want you to look successful, particularly in the money-management business. You have to have some trappings or signs of affluence, because your clients expect you to be successful. 'What, I'm going to give my money to someone who doesn't look successful?' I find it very uncomfortable."

But you won't give it up? You'll still live in the money world.

"You can change the world a lot more quickly with a checkbook. You can change the world over a longer period of time through activism. But a checkbook in the world draws people's attention . . . "

What you take in, you give out. The tide never stops. The waves never end. Some things wash away. They land at the bottom of an ocean or get buried under the sands of a beach. They are still there, though.

Remembrance. "My daughter died. And people go through their whole lives chasing whatever and doing things that they don't want to do and never realizing that life is terribly, terribly short—and it can be snatched at any moment. Grab, reach, take, snatch, move forward, get what you want . . . Money has enormous power. Money can attract people who can do good things."

It can't save people, even small children. What's money to them?

"Money is numbers. Money is dollars. Money is winning the game. That's how the money-management community thinks. If I lost X but another manager or the market was down 2X, then I'm doing good. I don't think that way. It's not about that. A lot of people are. They think money makes them better."

Kids don't care about money. It's not a concept in their minds.
Feed me, hug me, hold me.

If coins were made only of compassion, money would be the arbiter of goodwill.

Dialogue: Me and My Imagination

"I have a question for you."

"What is it?"

"You state that reality holds the key to balance, that I breed volatility. However, there are things—that only I can imagine—that bring us the most peace. The arbiter of goodwill is really me. Sure, I can be cloaked in money. I can take on different means: charity, philanthropy, service of some kind. I can imagine all sorts of ways to do good."

"I'm smiling now."

"Because I'm right?"

"Because it's the total utilization of you, plus the maximum consciousness of truth and reality, that gets us to another level—the ultimate level—of satisfaction."

"Self-realization, which I still can't imagine by the way."

"Instead of dragging you to another interview, let me just tell you what Brother Achalananda, a monk at the Self-Realization Fellowship in Los Angeles told me: 'Basically everybody is the same in terms of their needs: Everybody wants to be happy. Nobody wants to be miserable. We all want to have one and avoid the other. How is that done? We have to recognize the power of money and material things. That they breed happiness. And then we have to recognize that they are extrinsic. Instead of real happiness, it's bliss that we should be seeking. Happiness has its opposite. Bliss has no opposite. Bliss is an absolute. That is the quality of God. That is where self realization resides.'"

"An absolute? Bubba, that word will only get you as far as a bottle of vodka with me."

"I know. Absolutes are something you don't have to fret over. They just are. They are deep constructs that reach far beyond you or reason or any other faculty of the mind. Indeed, they are like the mind's atomic structure."

"Okay, I guess I'll just have to give you that one, then."

"Maybe this will help. Brother Achalananda also told us this: All the good and philanthropic works of the world, all noble successes, have to be accomplished through money. No saint ever lived who did not use money, directly or indirectly. But to acquire it without greed or attachment, and to use it rightly, is a great paradox and riddle of life. To love money is to be lost. That is the snare. You must use it wisely, allowing just the right voltage of prosperity to shine through the bulb of your life."

"I imagine he's investigated this a bit."

"He's been a monk for more than forty years. He is held out as an expert on the principles of self-realization and has lectured extensively around the world. When I finally asked Brother Achalananda specifi- cally what money means, he gives me an example: 'The family man has to earn money to support his family. He starts a certain business and begins to attend to the details that will make it successful. Now, what often happens after time? The business goes on successfully, and money perhaps accumulates, until there is much more than is necessary for the fulfillment of his wants and those of his family. Now, one of two things happens. Either money comes to be earned for its own sake, and a peculiar pleasure comes to be felt in hoarding; or, it may happen that the hobby of running this business for its own sake persists or increases all the more. We see that, in either case, the means of quelling original wants—which was the end—has become an end in itself; money or business has become the end . . . Then the purpose for which we apparently started a business becomes sec- ondary to the creation.'"

"I can imagine people losing sight of their goals, getting wrapped up in some job they originally took on temporarily to pay the bills, and then slowly giving up on their dreams."

"That's why some of us are frustrated, some of us dream of riches, some of us merely forget our goals and remain unconscious. It takes a brave person to change and seek self-realization. 'Change is pain,' Brother Achalananda reminds us. 'Even good change is pain,' he says."

"I'm imagining us sitting at that place again, the gazebo near the lake
where we spoke with Brother Achalananda."
"Yes, Brother Achalananda was happy to be at the Lake Shrine, too. Part
of Mahatma Gandhi's ashes are entombed there."
"I can imagine what Gandhi would have said about all this—our investi-
gation into what money means for you and me."
"For us, probably, integration: the total integration of the body, mind, and
spirit. See, until now, we've just focused on what money is, and what
money means to different demographic and psychographic groups.
We haven't explored what money ought to mean."
"I imagine we're going to look into that."
"It's the last series of inquiries. It's where both you and I will be confronted
by a different part of us—our deep, silent partner: Spirit."
"Sometimes I'm afraid of Spirit."
"Why is that?"
"Because he decides our fate, you know."
"No, I don't. That's why I want to ask people who know more about the
spirit than we do."
"Let's call for the chariot then."
"Yes, it's time to go."

The Spiritual Attachment of Money: What Money Should Mean

CHAPTER 22

The Search for Bliss

Spiritualism's dichotomy is inherent in the concept of money: At once it is a path to freedom and a barrier to free will.

Hope is the middle ground. And spirit, with all its might, tries to lift hope out of the trenches of mankind toward idealism.

If money is, as someone once said, a frozen desire, then both the suppression of desire and the manifestation of desire are governed not only by the psychological, but the spiritual paths we choose (or choose to ignore).

It's those spiritual paths that often pave the way to how we conduct ourselves in society.

Spiritual laws help us determine good from bad, right from wrong, and teach a code of ethics and morals. Spiritual laws, or universal laws, are those to which common laws, or societal laws, extrapolate their direction. Both govern our actions.

Money is fuel for our actions. But in which direction do we go? What will happen to us when we get there? And how can we find comfort along the way?

To be sure, money isn't the golden chalice. Money isn't the end *and* the means.

Spirit decidedly puts money in its proper place when the big issues arise— meaning of life and meaning of death issues.

Where and how, then—during normal times—should money be utilized for appreciation to gain its utmost value according to religious virtues?

Organized orders of religion lay the groundwork for what money ought to mean.

"The success of our lives and our future depends on our motivation and determination or self-confidence," says the Dalai Lama.

Money is, as it's said, the Great Motivator. Money is a provider of self-confidence. But money, most spiritual orders will agree, should be an incidental factor in our lives.

A small cult here in the United States has put money as its god. The group has money worship services, built money temples. But money isn't a god. Money may have godlike tendencies, but it isn't everlasting. Just ask any Internet entrepreneur.

We use money as an excuse for "it's okay." It's acceptance.

I want to buy that. It's okay. Money is accepted. But the big wants, the big hopes, dreams and desires can't be had with money. We can't buy our way out of dying. We can't buy our way into love. Money's role is limited in that way, just as those big questions are limited in our lives. Who wants to go around asking 'what does it all mean?' when all we're really trying to do is order a cheeseburger? Contemplating meaning isn't always practical.

Jack Miles, in his Pulitzer Prize–winning book *God: A Biography*,[16] argues that the biggest proof of our search for the existence of God, comes from our attempts to model ourselves after God—most blatantly in the West, where Judeo-Christian mores most lie.

"They believed that by trying they could make themselves into better copies of the divine original, and they bent themselves diligently to the task. *Imitatio Dei*, the imitation of God, was a central category in Jewish piety. The imitation of Christ, God made man, was equally central to Christians," Miles writes.

Why model ourselves after something that no one has ever seen? We want to trade on that hope that we, too, will someday be godlike. Until then, commercialism and materialism placate, empowered by money.

The two worlds—spiritualism and materialism—don't mix. Otherwise, JESUS SAVES would be a testimonial advertisement for a bank.

There are more than three thousand orders of faith in the world. There are about twenty-two widely practiced religions and twelve classical world religions—Baha'i, Buddhism, Christianity, Confucianism, Hinduism, Islam, Jainism, Judaism, Shinto, Sikhism, Taoism, and Zoroastrianism—to which people turn to most for answers, according to the Adherents organization, duly noting that every human is: (a) like all other humans, (b) like some other humans, and (c) like no other human.

Sociocultural influences probably direct the course of money the most in the context of human nature. Consumerism after all is bred outside religious orders (unless you're trying to sell God, or are part of the 14 percent of the world population that is nonreligious). But religions do have their say. And money is often at odds with—arguably in competition with—their goals.

Money in Christianity is the root of all evil. Money in Islam caused Mohammed to head for the mountain. Yet money can do good.

"[Money] takes us out of innocent idealism and brings us into the deeper, more soulful places where power, prestige and self-worth are hammered out through substantial involvement in the making of culture. Therefore, money can give grounding and grit to a soul that otherwise might fade in the soft pastels of innocence," writes Thomas Moore in *Care of the Soul.*[17]

Money's false promise is that it is a protector of the soul. That is the job of spirit. Such are the two sides to the coin.

In the corporeal sense, money may play the role of God—deciding what type of life we will lead. But the role of god stretches further. That is why the U.S. dollar comes with a disclaimer: IN GOD WE TRUST. Hence, we turn to religion for some answers that go beyond the practical, psychological, and sociological attachments of money.

The religions chosen represent those most recognized and celebrated in the West. There are subsets of each, of course. There are many leaders of each, too, of course. But just as the rest of this book has pulled from myriad ranks of society, so will we follow that pattern into the spiritual world.

CHAPTER 23

Money in the Muslim World

A black head-veil. Long, dark strands of hair are pulled back over her ears spilling just over her shoulders. Her brown eyes are piercing. Her intensity is apparent.

Dr. Hasnita Dato Hashim is standing in an airport in Riyadh, Saudi Arabia, speaking to me about the Islamic perspective on money.

"Someone making money at the expense of someone else losing money is not accepted," she says.

Dr. Hasnita is widely considered an expert on Islamic principles governing money and trade. She speaks around the world on Shari'ah, the Islamic interpretation of the Koran governing banking and finance. She meets with Muslim clerics, political leaders, and business executives to shed light on what is acceptable in the eyes of Islam and what isn't, when it comes to monetary ethics. She has begun a Web site, IslamiQ, for Muslim investors, explaining what is ethically deemed right and wrong when it comes to money matters. And she manages investment funds based on her religious beliefs.

That fact that Dr. Hasnita is a woman conferring with leaders in the traditionally male-dominated Muslim religion is a sign of the changing times in the world of Islam.

It's so alien to us Westerners.

Take Riyadh. Men dress in *thawbs*, a full-length shirt, and affix a *ghutra*, a cord-coiled cotton headdress. Women must wear a black cloak and veil when they leave their homes. There is no eating pork or drinking alcohol. Everything revolves around religious dos and religious don'ts in Saudi Arabia, a country that houses a desert the size of France, a country that houses Islam's two holiest cities, Mecca and Medina, a country that houses some of the richest people in the world on account of its vast oil reserves.

Dr. Hasnita's job is to try to make sense out of the religious laws and customs for the 1.3 billion Muslims in the world. After all, Muslims live in the West (between 6 and 7 million in the United States alone), visit the West, conduct commerce with the West. They need to integrate. They need to be able to buy, sell, invest—trade, like every one else.

Islamic laws prohibit the taking of interest. That makes banking a problem. Islamic laws also prohibit trade merely for the sake of making money. That rules out investing.

Dr. Hasnita has enlisted the help of religious scholars to help her interpret Islamic laws in a way that leaves room for commercialism.

"In Islam, the use of money is different than in the traditional banking system, where profit is encouraged and commercialism is encouraged," says Dr. Hasnita.

She has the voice of a medical doctor, although she has a Ph.D. It's just one of those voices that is firm, but caring. Unlike some people who speak with a Semitic dialect, she avoids the lingering verbal question mark at the end of sentence. She is exact in her choice of words. She seems, actually, always in a bit of a rush.

"In Islam, you make money for the benefit of everyone, " says Dr. Hasnita.

That isn't capitalism. And it makes trade in today's global village very difficult.

But there are ways to live within the laws of Islam and still make money, trade, and invest. Here's how: "If you invest in a good company with an underlying asset, that can be okay," Dr. Hasnita says. "The risks then are based on the value of something—you both stand the chance of losing. We can't allow someone to make money and allow someone else to lose everything. That is inequitable."

Now, we're getting somewhere. Dr. Hasnita emphasizes the "can be okay." It's the qualifier, and where the laws of Islam get complex.

Murabahah refers to a particular kind of sale where a seller agrees with a buyer to provide a certain amount of profit relative to an initial cost. Everything is disclosed, including the original costs and the profit, which can be a lump sum or a percentage. It's okay to trade that way in the eyes of Islam.

Musharakah is an Arabic word meaning "to share." It's used in business and trade, so that partners share the profit or loss of a venture. Because interest is prohibited in Islamic law, if a debtor suffers a loss, the creditor can't claim a fixed rate of return or earn a high rate of profit. People have to profit or lose money together in any trade or venture in the eyes of Islam.

Such laws make it cumbersome at best to operate in the capital markets today. So, Shari'ah experts have come up with a "5 percent rule" that deems it "tolerable" to deal with companies that have a maximum level of 5 percent of non–Shari'ah compliant activities or "tainted income sources." This makes it okay to invest or engage in trade or commerce.

Tainted income sources don't just mean investments. They include banking—financial institutions make or pay interest—and companies that have any association with pork products. So, don't look for your friendly, next-door Muslim to be working at your local bank or deli. Still, Dr. Hasnita sees a change in the way Muslims are integrating with the West. Already, about $150 billion has moved into the Western capital markets from Muslim coffers. And that amount is growing 20 to 30 percent per year.

Dr. Hasnita says, "We are looking to make a difference and change the world."

How? Through the ethical maneuvering of money via the capital markets, according to the ways of Islam.

With a hold on one-quarter of the world's population, Muslims exhibit a huge potential audience for Western culture. The obstacles, of course, are what's allowed and how these material items will affect the Islamic culture in the future.

Dr. Hasnita is a case in point. Being a woman sends a strong sign to the West that traditional Western conceptions of Islam should be rethought.

"I am received well, even in traditional Islamic countries," says Dr. Hasnita. "Because I'm a woman, they are proud. It shows we are modern."

My Imagination interrupts: "An image I can't seem to shake loose is of a man wearing a turban. This man is sitting. He has a black shawl wrapped over his shoulders. A long beard points down in V-shape to his chest. While it's just an image, I can't help but sense that he is religious."

Religion. It's evident in everything a Muslim does, from the way he or she speaks, to the way he or she dresses, to the way he or she eats, even to the way he or she spends money. Religion isn't something that is reserved for one day in the week. Prayer times are posted on IslamiQ's Web site: early morning, sunrise, noontime, late afternoon, just before sunset, and just after sunset—at specific times, precise to the minute. Five times a day, every day.

In Egypt, during Ramadan, the Muslim high holiday, I observed liquor being taken down from shelves, people scurrying home before sunset, the calls to prayer that stopped traffic and had people on their knees before the Nile River.

It stops, this religion. It forbids, it bans, it seeks retribution. All this is in the name of Allah, or God.

This is how it began: In the early years of the seventh century, an Arab merchant from the city of Mecca named Muhammad ibn Abdallah took his family on retreat to a nearby mountain. He was part of the Quraysh Bedouin tribe, who had become quite wealthy as Mecca became the central trading spot for Arabia. Tribal values had changed as capitalism thrived for the Quraysh, and it was quickly making a new religion of money. According to Karen

Armstrong in her book *A History of God: The 4000-year Quest of Judaism, Christianity, and Islam*[18] the Quraysh felt money had "saved" it from the perils of nomadic life, cushioning its members from malnutrition and tribal violence, where they faced the possibility of extinction.

Muhammad believed the new religion was going to tear the tribe apart morally and politically unless it could put another value at its center and overcome all the greed and egotism that its new wealth had brought. This was probably on his mind, Armstrong posits, when he sat in prayer on the summit of Mount Hira. He would have been praying, by the way, to al-Lah, "the God"—the same God as the one worshipped at the time by Christians and Jews.

Suddenly, an angel appeared.

"Recite!" the angel commanded. (*Iqra!*). And the rest of the scripture is called the *qur'an*—literally translated from the Arabic as "the Recitation"; it took twenty-three years.

The Koran comprises the verses as told to Muhammad by the angel Gabriel, who is also God's communicator in the Bible.

Money, or the way you conduct yourself in business, isn't as big a part of the Koran as it is the Bible. Mostly, the Koran is a series of verses fashioned as metaphors to exemplify the way to heaven. Money, in the eyes of Islam, can't get you there.

Money, says Dr. Hasnita "doesn't belong to you, but it's something that God has given to you and your neighbors. Some people will have more money and more wealth than others. We have designed a system to limit this and to limit the greed in a person. Through hard work and productivity, there's no reason you can't be wealthy. And that's not just about the money." She says in Islam you must contribute back to society in order to enlighten others (a principle known as *zakah*). It's like a tax for the poor and the needy and the education of others. "You need some form of currency to purchase goods and services. But that's not the point. We look at how you distribute your wealth."

Sure, in strict religious countries there may not be the same type of value put on money like there is here in the United States. Money is viewed more as a responsibility in Islam. Every action is broken down like that; Allah governs. In the West, we really don't view money as a responsibility. Dr. Hasnita's job is to bridge the two worlds.

She points out the rise in socially conscious and ethical investing. (One out of every $8 invested in the United States goes into an investment with a social or environmental concern. The total amount of assets under management in this category come to more than $2 trillion, the Social Investment Forum says.) She says there is a new consciousness awakening in the West, one more akin to the ways Muslims conduct themselves—responsibly.

And there is something to be said about that. Having a good conscience about every action you make imputes ethics into every decision, from the smallest to the largest. There is a direct connection there, and it makes you feel, of course, like you're not alone. I can understand the comfort in that. But at the same time, I can see the suffocation such strictness could bring.

Freedom, in every manner, is the hallmark of Western culture. In the Islamic culture, you are only free when you are in heaven.

My Imagination is flashing an image of Atlas, chained to the planet. He is bigger than the world, yet constrained by it. The universe, all black, is dotted with tiny, bright stars. They are the eyes of heaven, my Imagination decides, looking down with great pity upon Atlas.

Ego, power, and influence are human forces. No matter how much wealth, power, or fame one acquires, they are inextricably tied to our humanity, our "human-ness."

Our actions, every action we take, is a reflection of God's will, a Muslim would say. When we exert wrong, we perpetuate wrong against all of mankind. When we are immoral, we make all of mankind immoral. When we bring evil into the world, we bring it into the world for everyone to bear.

"Whosoever receives an admonition from his Lord and stops eating Riba (usury) shall not be punished for the past; his case is for Allah (to judge); but whoever returns [to Riba], such are the dwellers of the Fire—they will abide therein," says the Koran.

Money, in Islamic terms, is the trust of God. On U.S. bills, it's written IN GOD WE TRUST. Between the two meanings is a world of difference.

The Muslim religion was begun as a rebellion against capitalism—its values, its moral undoings. Today, in radical elements, it's not much different. We have seen the wrath of radical Muslim elements waging war against the United States. We have seen, up close and personal, the destruction. How much more emblematic can the attack on the World Trade Center be?

Make no mistake, it's a war on money and its values and principles. Morality and money are the two things Islam was built upon, respectively for and against.

Of course, money itself isn't the harbinger of immorality. Money, after all, is a reflection of who we really are as people. And it's a mecca for that.

Dialogue: Me and My Imagination

"I never imagined that Islam was begun as a religion against money."

"Looks that way."

"So I imagine that's why there is such an anti-Western movement among them."

"Not everyone, and we have to be careful here. The radical elements who have struck out with violence and force against the 'capitalist imperialists' are a very small minority of Muslims."

"We seem so different. Our values, our dress, our manners . . . almost everything."

"Again, not as much as you'd imagine. Remember, the angel Gabriel who spoke to Muhammad is the same angel who is the communicator in the Bible. So, Christians and Jews share that same belief. It separates after Christ separated the Christians from the Jews. In fact, Muslims believe Jesus was a prophet—just not the messiah."

"Yes, I can imagine how religions share commonality. Their interpretations of morals, from whichever oracle, must be similar. There is only one right and one wrong."

"One right? One wrong? Moral absolutes? I'm not so sure about that. What is sure is the place of money in society—it is something to do good with. From a religious point of view, anyway. From that perspective, money, like all things, is possessed by God."

"One God."

"Yes."

"When I imagine God, I imagine some bearded man sitting on a throne looking down upon the earth."

"There's no sense trying to imagine what I can't experience. It doesn't work, has a false ring to it. Muslims, actually, say they can't describe what God is, so they set about describing what God isn't."

"That sparks negativity in me."

"It shouldn't. When you imagine God, there is some judgment usually associated with the image."

"That's you, something you picked up somewhere. I'll admit, some of my imaginations do give you some pause. Although, there are many more times when what I imagine in that vein gives you some comfort."

"I know, and intellectually I know that there should be no reason for either of those things. However, it's inexplicable."

"Meantime, I'm left wondering about all the things we take for granted. If we were Muslim, we couldn't do a lot of the things we do."

"If we were really a practicing Muslim, that's true. I'd have a whole different value system from which I'd have raised you, for instance."

"So, our dreams would be different?"

"Of course. Materially speaking, that is. Money isn't something to compete for—it's the underlying principles that are of value. If you gain money from, say interest, you'd be required to give it away."

"I can't imagine doing that. But then again I can't imagine wearing a nightshirt walking around during the day either."

"Joking aside, you're imagining what we see as the image of the Islamic community. Granted, some of that is true, but it's changing. People are becoming more 'modern.' They are embracing more and more of the freer values of the West."

"Isn't that what this violence is all about? I imagine the radicals could see the United States as the new Mecca."

"Indeed."

"And what about money?"

"What about it?"

"As a value. Is it used the same way as we use it here? I mean, you have to work, right? You have to buy things, clothe yourself, all that. Then what?"

"From the perspective of abundance, you have to give it back. Don't get me wrong, you could live a nice comfortable life, have nice things, but you'd be expected to also support your local neighborhood or society. You'd be expected to do business with local, Muslim businesses. Then, there's charity. A Muslim should practice *zakah*."

"Gesundheit. So, tell me, what is this charity thing you're speaking of?"

"All righty, then. Here we go again: *Zakah* refers to the purification of a Muslim's wealth and soul. Wealth purification is using money for justified distribution. Purification of the soul means freedom from hatred, jealousy, selfishness, greed . . . "

"Sounds serious."

"It is. *Zakah* is one the five pillars of Islam. The other pillars are the profession of faith, daily prayers, fasting, and pilgrimage to Mecca. So, *zakah* is considered an important economic tool in an Islamic state or society. Every Muslim at the end of the year who is 'in possession of the equivalent of eight-five grams of gold or more in cash or articles of trade,' must pay his or her *zakah* at least 2.5 percent of that amount. This is supposed to prevent hoarding wealth and advocates solidarity among Muslims; excess wealth is distributed to the poor."

"Okay, enough, you win."

"Thank you."

"Well, I, for one, am beginning to imagine the Islamic world as one big family. And they choose to keep everything in it."

"That's about right. There is a system they use called *hawala*—a Hindi term, actually, but it's used by a great deal of Muslims."

"Hiawatha, what? Now I'm picturing an American Indian girl."

"*Hawala* is your word."

"Keep it coming, Webster."

"Literally translated, that's what *hawala* means: 'your word.'"

"Oh, why didn't you just say so?"

"Sometimes it takes turns at the plate to knock one through to you."

"B . . . a . . . s . . . e . . . b . . . a . . . l . . . l . . . "

"Back to money."

"Right, and *hawala*. We don't have such a thing in the West."

"Not yet. And we'll get to that bit later. We used to trade on our word, but not now. We operate on a different system, more influenced by Christian and Judaic values."

"Show me the money!"

"Stop."

"Okay, I'm subjective. But I have been trained to imagine that Jews and Christians even treat money differently."

"Is that so?"

"Yes. I can imagine more about Jews and money than Christians and money. You've been exposed to a lot more influences on that subject."

"I know. Most of it is ignorant comment."

"Care to clean up your imagination?"

"Why don't I leave that job for a rabbi?"

CHAPTER 24

Money in the Jewish World

Rabbi Burt Visotszky and I meet in front of the Jewish Theological Seminary on the Upper West Side of Manhattan. The building is essentially on the grounds of Columbia University. It's way up there, as New Yorkers say, on 122nd Street and Broadway.

The front of the JTS is under construction. It had been in disrepair since the 1970s, Rabbi Visotszky tells me. Rabbi Visotszky goes by Burt. He doesn't wear his religious nature on his sleeve. He is dressed in an open-collared shirt and slacks. No yarmulke.

Rabbi Burt explains that a fire had destroyed much of the front hall, but fire codes and most of all a lack of money had kept the seminary from rebuilding or repairing it.

"It was of no other use, so we used it as a lobby. Then we decided recently that something had to be done," Rabbi Burt says.

The JTS embarked on a plan to fix the front entrance and model a lobby. What it needed, of course, was the funding to do it.

"A development person got a call from an old rabbi in Nebraska. He wanted to donate part of his estate after he died to the seminary," says Rabbi Burt, reciting the story as we wind around a maze of construction and take a small elevator to his small office. I figure he is recounting the tale just to buy time until we could sit down more formally. But the story about the front entrance is more than that, it's the theme that Rabbi Burt uses in his later discussion with me. Amid rows of books on the Talmud and the Torah, he continues.

"The rabbi and his wife flew in to New York. They came here. They sat down with the development person. And, to give her credit, she said, 'Rabbi, why don't you do something good with your money right now, something you can see?' Now, this was a rabbi from Nebraska who had spent his whole life in the rabbinical order. How much money could he have? Anyway, he says, 'What do you have in mind?' And the development person says, 'Why don't you donate your money to help us fix the front entrance?' And the rabbi asks, 'How much will that cost?' And the development person says, "$7 million.' The rabbi looked at his wife. She nodded. And the rabbi said, 'Done.'"

This rabbi, as it happens, had moved to Omaha in the late-1960s. His wife had written a children's book. The financier Warren Buffett and his wife had read the book. They liked it, and soon the wives became fast friends. Warren Buffett took all the rabbi's money at that time, some $60,000, and invested it.

Warren Buffett is one of the world's most successful investors. Ten thousand dollars invested with him in 1965 would equal about $50 million today. Needless to say, the rabbi from Omaha could well afford to fix the front entrance to the JTS.

The story about the front entrance gives Rabbi Burt and me a jumping-off point to begin our discussion about what money really means in the context of Judaism. Rabbi Burt often speaks for the rabbinical order, rendering ethical and moral opinions on everything from public policy to politics. He has spoken at the request of former President Bill Clinton and on many international panels to provide the "Jewish view." With the backdrop of a story on what money can do, Rabbi Burt talks to me about what money is and what money should be.

He says, "Speaking as a rabbi and from the Jewish tradition, money is another means by which you have the opportunity to make choices about the type of human being you're going to be. Which is to say, what money you have and how you use it is a way in determining who you are.

"In the rabbinical system, you can use it to do God's Commandments, or you can use it for less noble purposes. In rabbinical law, in Torah law, all capital belongs to God."

Those words echo: All capital belongs to God. I use the big "G" here in deference to whom I'm interviewing.

I, I should now note, was raised Catholic, traveled the paths of Buddhism, Hinduism, and even converted to Judaism, but rest between agnosticism and atheism, depending on the day. On some days I'd like to thank god. On other days I'd like to curse him or her or them—whatever. Trouble is, you can never find a god when you need one.

As even the Bible says, "Seek ye the Lord while He may be found, call ye upon Him while He is near. But He is far away."

And it's the Bible where the answers to what money means can be found. So says Rabbi Burt.

"There's a verse of scripture that says *Li Ha Kesef A Li A Zahev*. 'Mine is the silver and Mine is the gold. This is the word of God.'

"What that means is that we recognize that all wealth is the gift of God. It's not really ours. It's ours only for a short while, and we have obligations.

"Charity is not something you do out of the goodness of your heart. Charity is a commandment. You must help your fellow man. You must donate a portion of your income.

"Since the ancient world was an agrarian society, they thought in terms of real estate and crop. You had to leave a portion of your crop for the poor. You could not harvest every corner of your field, you always left a corner for the poor. And it's not like you were leaving it for the poor. It *belonged* to the poor.

"They have their share of your land because it's God's land, in the end. In terms of the actual cash you have, that, too, you're obligated to support certain institutions, whether it's supporting the poor, feeding the hungry, clothing the naked. Those are all biblical commands."

I don't need to prod Rabbi Burt with many questions. In fact, I have just asked him the one. He waxes on cogently. Compelling him is probably more time than it is my subject matter. He only has about an hour for me; he and his wife are driving to upstate New York to participate in a cancer walk.

Before I can even ask him to exemplify, he tells me yet another story.

"There's a very famous story of two rabbis going on their way to the bath houses in the afternoon. Living as they did in the Roman world, they did as the Romans did and they went to the bath houses. And on the way in, as it was not uncommon, there was a beggar outside. And they said, 'We'll take care of you on the way out.' And when they came out, they found him dead. And they were mortified that by perhaps not giving him money for food, they had cost him his life. So they said, 'Look, while we didn't care for him while he was alive, let us at least make sure that he gets a proper burial.' And when they went to take care of the body, they found around his neck a bag of gold coins. And they realized that they weren't responsible for his death at all, that he was quite comfortably off. Which caused one of the rabbis to say, 'Thank God that there are amongst us those who seek charity, deceivers.' Which is a very odd statement . . . "

Uh, yeah—I'm starting to have to edit Rabbi Burt. And he was doing so well on his own. My Imagination, of course, is off somewhere in the old Roman bath houses, flouncing around an indoor pool, ogling women in togas serving grapes. Meanwhile, I'm here editing text, trying to paraphrase Rabbi Burt, who, I think, means to say that because we occasionally turn beggars away, it's a good thing a few of them don't really need our charity.

My Imagination is calling me to write more about the Roman baths, but I am dissuading him. This deceiver section—"No, go away! Yes, I see her!"— is difficult. Does this mean that God plays tricks on us to test our compassion? Does this mean that the rich should give away their wealth? If we all gave to every beggar, would we ourselves go broke? How much is enough? Bottom line, "The rule is you help the needy." But, and I'll turn back to Rabbi Burt for this, "The rabbis have no problem in being comfortable for yourself."

That's just great. What if I like a lot of comfort and have no room for charity? Well, that's no good either.

Get out of the pool, please. Towel off. We're getting to some good stuff and I need all of my concentration.

"The Torah itself talks about tithing. Tithing means one-tenth. But if you actually go back and add up all the different tithes, it comes out to as much as 12 to 15 percent of your income going to biblical causes, whether it's supporting the poor or supporting institutional religion," Rabbi Burt says.

This seems like a lot of money to me. Taxing someone's income and tying it to a commandment has an implied "or else." And I say this to Rabbi Burt. He agrees. "There is an 'or else,'" he admits. "But it's part of the religion. Look, to me it's part of a piece of ethics that is redolent of a modern philosopher named John Rawls, who's up at Harvard. And Rawls came up with a theory of justice. And Rawls's theory is that you have to create a system of justice where people are in agreement with the following proviso: You could wake up on any given morning in that society and be any other member of that society. So because of that proviso, you always want to take sure that there's the maximum amount of fairness distributed. In a way, that's what the rabbis are saying."

Rabbi Burt tells me that the rabbis didn't flagrantly make this stuff up. In the Talmud, he notes, an entire chapter is devoted to commodities trading. Another chapter is about interest. "The Torah prohibits Jews from taking interest from one another," he says. Loans, therefore, had to be equated to value. Value is, of course, what money represents.

"They have a very complex trading system. They lived in the Roman World. And because of their market consciousness, I think that they really understand money as another commodity. Food is a commodity. And each of those commodities can be used for good or for ill.

"For the rabbis, how you use those commodities was a measure of who you were and how you, and in the rabbinical ideal, how you would be judged by God."

And, that's how he ends it, Rabbi Burt's and my discussion of money.

My Imagination has covered up at the word "judged" and the word "God." He is creeping out of the bath house now, out into the ancient world. As He carefully shuts the stone door, the last sounds of laughter echo. The last splashes from the pool are muffled. I, according to Him, am there now, carrying my sandals. My toga isn't quite wrapped properly. My hair is wet and tousled.

I turn from the door. A beggar is standing to the side, his hand out in front of me. My Imagination has decided that I don't have a coin or anything of value on me. I take the beggar's hand in mine. He clasps it tight. I hand him my shoes and walk off down a dusty road, barefoot. I am soiled as the wind blows and lifts the dirt from the road into the air. It swirls and rings and sticks to the wet spots on my skin. I don't mind. You see, I can wash again.

What snaps me back to reality is the lesson of washing again. It occurs to me that just as the Muslims disallow the taking of interest as usury, the Jews did too. But instead of devising a system of "acceptable" places to put your money, as the Muslims do, the Jews made money itself the commodity. Therefore, with money as a value, an agreeable term could be set out on which to receive payment for that value. Banking, of course, derived from this; diamond dealing, of course, derived from this. All because the Jews weren't allowed to own property in many countries in certain periods of time in history. Also, they were a migratory group of people who didn't have a homeland to settle in until fifty years ago. This made portable wealth and trading, like diamond dealing, a lasting trade.

The idea of value within the Jewish religion is of utmost importance. Why? Because it is a symbol of worth. When, as Edouard Valdman writes in his fine book *Jews and Money: Toward a Metaphyics of Money*,[19] "Gaining money from money was the height of abomination, and only abominable people could engage in such activity," he is saying that respectability was gained, power was gained, through the force that money brought with it. A truth was there. A truth, that despite what the West said, money was worthy, that Jews themselves were worthy.

After centuries of being castigated and discriminated against, value and self-worth became entwined with the physical manifestation of those measures—money.

To be sure, money is important to all of us. But it's most important because it can buy a sense of belonging, a sense of security. I could see how one would want to relish that value.

I am beginning to see now how money truly is a reflection of self-worth.

Dialogue: Me and My Imagination

"You're a racist."

"What are you talking about?"

"Anti-Semitic, swastika-wearing, skinhead-lovin', Jew-hatin' racist."

"Excuse me?"

"I can imagine how you calling Jews the same things as money would set off firerockets in that community."

"Please, I said we are the same, we all are the same."

"Oh, then just get me straight here. Jews, in your extremely prejudiced point of view, have reason to place a higher value on money because they were discriminated against?"

"Are discriminated against. My point was, first, that Jews see money from a religious perspective as something to give away to the community to help others. Everyone's dough. Then, my point was to show how much value they placed on money for the purposes of security, comfort, community binds, and so on."

"Binds? I'm picturing leather straps."

"Anyway, all I was about to say was that hoarding is sinful in the Jewish faith. Determining value, on the other hand, is very much respected."

"And?"

"Here's the thing. Jesus was a Jew, right?"

"I never imagined that he was."

"Well, he was. Wasn't much choice back then. And what was it all about? What was the purpose of his arrival, the significance?"

"History wasn't my bag . . . "

"To save mankind."

"From whom?"

"From ourselves."

"Me? What did I do?"

"We had placed such little value on our lives that we were corrupt, sloths, mongers."

"So, now I imagine you're saying that Jesus saved us. In fact, I'm picturing a cute, little bumper sticker like that now: JESUS SAVES."

"I know how it sounds. So, cut it out. Look, I'm not saying that Jesus was the Messiah. I'm also not saying he wasn't. I'm merely saying that theoretically his *raison d'etre*—"

"Back to French again, which leaves me blank—"

"—his *raison d'etre*—and, again, theoretically—was to symbolize that man had the potential to be good. That we, as humans, were of value, but that we had to begin to respect ourselves, start to take responsibility for ourselves."

"Can I imagine an 'Or what?' I mean, if we are in control of our own destiny, then who cares if we became irresponsible?"

"Ah, you beautiful, impressionable little baby boy. That is the point. Jesus was around—again supposedly—to show that someone does care, that we aren't in control of our destiny."

"And the 'Or what?'"

"That we are worthy, worthy of the Creator."

"Again—and listen, now: *Or what*?"

"Okay, I get you. Well, remember that book I read and which sparked all sorts of images for you to run with—*The Inferno*? That's the 'Or what.'"

"Yikes . . . We're back to that moral stuff again aren't we?"

"More. We're talking about our value, our own sense of money—how we make the world grow into a better place—by exerting our will."

"A will to me is a piece of parchment scrolled into cone that is suddenly unfolded and read aloud by an attorney in a frock coat."

"You, my friend, are an example of our will. You are an example of our morality, our base assumptions about how we should conduct our lives."

"And spend our money?"

"That conclusion is fast approaching. You indeed may play the most significant part or the least—depending upon how the world turns out."

"Back to that Jesus thing again? Or are we now talking flames, fire, and brimstone, again?

"The cold, hard question of reason is, Is the world a better place?"

"Than?"

"No 'than.' Just now. By using our moral, intellectual and physical capital goods, have we made the world the best place it can be?"

"I'd have to imagine not, given all the things I can imagine."

"When more than a billion people live on less than $1 per day? When more than 10 million children die of preventable diseases each year? When more than 100 million children do not attend school? Or when more than half a million women die unnecessarily each year during pregnancy or childbirth? I'd say not, too."

"I can only imagine religion is there to serve the pain in your world and help you deal with reality."

"Exactly. So, it's time to look at the largest of all faiths, where most people in the world look for hope."

CHAPTER 25

Money in the Christian World

It is easier for a camel to pass through the eye of a needle than for a
rich man to enter the Kingdom of God.

—Matthew 19:24

T hat's a bold proposition, considering that there are more than a
billion Catholics in the world
who would believe such a thing. More than 300 million Christians besides
them, represented by eighty-five different sects, would also have to believe that
scripture from the New Testament. What with our global society turning more
and more toward a system of riches for *everyone*, dire consequences seem to be
forthcoming.

Yet, there is a balance, even if Matthew also says, "You cannot serve both
God and money."

The most frequently discussed topic, or the topic the apostles and gospel-
writers wished to address most in the New Testament, is money. It is refer-
enced more than any other item, according to Biblical scholars. Why?
Commercialism and trade had proliferated in the ancient world.

The values brought by commerce: Greed, sloth, gluttony, and so on, were
to be rejected. Hence, the coming of the savior Jesus Christ.

Today, there is still greed, there is still sloth, there is still gluttony. The workings of capitalism breed such destructive forces. The Christian way to work within
the context of this framework isn't to reject money and capitalism, it's to "do unto
others as they would do unto you." Of course when competition is involved, that
maxim gets complex. It calls into question modern ethics. To get some real
answers to ethical questions about money in the context of Christianity, I turn
to one of the men the world's largest religion turns to: Father Benedict Groeschel.

A bit on Father Benedict: Director of the Office for Spiritual Development of the Archdiocese of New York, he is considered a "spiritual guide." Father Benedict founded the Franciscan Friars of the Renewal in the South Bronx and is a professor at St. Joseph's seminary in Yonkers. The author of some fourteen books on the spirit, he specializes and lectures widely on Christian ethics.

There you go. Now, let's put on the unofficial stuff: He was Mother Theresa's confessor. He is sought after by church leaders for advice on everything from psychology to prayers. He travels the globe. He is smart, affable, an eloquent orator. He is like a Christian goodwill ambassador at large.

I begin my inquisition with the simple question of what money means.

"Money is a means to an end, it's never an end to itself. Money is the opportunity to have goods, or abilities, or even powers to help other people fulfill their responsibility before God, and to have a decent life, and to fulfill one's own responsibilities before God," Father Benedict tells me.

He has a white beard, wears a gray wool sack of a robe tied by a rope. He could exist in any century. Well, okay, he was wearing sneakers.

We're at the Trinity House, a retreat center in New York. It's a beautiful place. It's by the bay. It rests among mansions in one of the wealthiest communities in the state: Larchmont. It's peaceful. It coexists. I recognize the symbolism of it all.

There are many questions to ask Father Benedict, so I decide to let the New Testament itself lead the way.

> If anyone has enough money to live well and sees a brother or sister in
> need and refuses to help, how can God's love be in that person?
> —1 John 3:17

"When possession of gold becomes a goal in itself, it is, as St. Paul said, 'the root of all evil.' I realize that I'm saying this in a capitalist society. And I don't mean this to apply as a political or economic system. I think any system can be corrupted by greed. In a kind of secular idealism, the very early Marxists thought they were going to take the very motive of greed and possession and power out of money. And they managed to create one of the greatest catastrophes in human history. You know, what they attempted to do in their classless society without wealth, what they managed to create, was an extremely militaristic culture that destroyed people because they had no money to protect themselves. Money is a protection of the poor. So, if you ask me, in my honest opinion, a moderated capitalism, which keeps from becoming complete piracy, is probably what works best. But it's not some great ideal," says Father Benedict.

[Jesus] told him: Go and sell all you have and give the money to the poor, and you will have treasure in heaven. Then come, follow me.
—Mark 10:21

In other words, give up all your possessions and you will be saved?

"I'm a disciple of Saint Augustine, and he never thought human history was going to be more than a mixed bag . . . [So] I don't look for the perfect system. I think there should be a free but vibrant system of responsibility for the poor who are cared for by the public system and, to some degree, by the private sector. But I must say that a society will always have the very poor, the humanly indigent kind of people who can't make it in the system, particularly if we have a system based on volunteerism. In a system of serfdom, you can fit everybody in, even if there is one guy whose job it is just to talk to the horses. In a free system, people are going to fall to the bottom. I'd say this is between 3 and 4 percent of any decent society. Next, you have the poor who can help themselves. This is the group of people who have often done well in the American system. People who get off the boat with little more than the shirt on their back. This accounts for maybe 10 percent of the population. Now, it's not the 4 percent but it's the 10 percent that need a little push . . . " Father Benedict says.

It's not giving it all up. It's giving some to those who need it most.

Jesus entered the Temple and began to drive out the merchants and their customers. He knocked over the tables of the money-changers and the stalls of those selling doves. He said: the scriptures declare that my Temple will be called a place of prayer, but you have turned it into a den of thieves.
—Matthew 21:12-17

"The great problem in this country was The Great Society. Mr. [President] Johnson made a very great mistake in confusing the poor with the very poor. So, they began to treat the poor like the very poor, and so your number of dependent people went from 4 percent to 14 percent—and you didn't do that 10 percent any earthly good," says Father Benedict.

Our culture supports those who don't need it; that's sinful.

Tell those who are rich in the world not to be proud and not to trust their money, which will soon be gone . . . tell them to use their money to do good. They should be rich in good works and give generously to those in need, always being ready to share with others.
—1 Timothy 6:17-18

"I'm a friar," Father Benedict says. "I took a vow of poverty."

My Imagination stops me from continuing further. He is at a loss to see how anyone in a modern environment can live without some form of money.

Father Benedict explains that his annual budget is $8 million. That means he has to raise $8 million to do good. Doing good, to him, is working with the poor. That gives back. That takes the very poor and pushes them into the class of the poor. That takes the poor and gives them hope of something more in their life. What he takes for himself isn't money for doing this. What he takes is another step toward heaven.

> . . . [P]eople who owned land and houses sold them and brought money to the Apostles to give to others in need.
> —Acts 4:34

I've begun to pry away the prongs of the Christian obsession over money. It's not about the people in need. It's about giving to the people in need. You can't change the circumstances life has already brought to bear. You can change the circumstances that life may bring. That's why money is solicited and money is distributed. A God connection from the rich to the poor is established.

"You get to the upper class, and they have surpluses, and here's where they can be very greedy. And it's the responsibility not only of religion but of other philanthropic organizations to teach people they must use a portion of their wealth to do good to others or they will be corrupted themselves," says Father Benedict.

The New Testament, too, addresses this:

> Look here, you rich people . . . your wealth is rotting away and your fine clothes are moth-eaten rags . . . the very wealth you were count-ing on will eat away your flesh in hell. The treasure you have accumu-lated will stand as evidence against you on the Day of Judgment. For listen! Hear the cries of the field-workers who you have cheated of their pay . . . the cries have reached the ears of the Lord almighty . . . you have condemned good people who had no power to defend them-selves against you.
> —James 5:1-6

In his Encyclical Letter the Chief Duties of Christians as Citizens, Pope Leo XIII adds, "[charity] binds intimately to God those whom it has embraced and with loving tenderness, causes them to draw their life from God, to act with God, to refer all the love of our neighbor, since men share in the infinite goodness of God and bear in themselves the impress of his image and likeness."

That was over a century ago. But the words hold even today. It is the image Christians seek. It is in God's image Christians hope to find happiness, says Father Benedict.

Reality is the magnifier of ugliness.

The thorny ground represents those who hear and accept the Good News, but all too quickly the message is crowded out by the cares of this world and the lure of wealth.
—Matthew 13:22

Money is something in the Christian faith that equates to stability, to balance. Right from wrong. Good from evil. The two forces must always be balanced.

"Those who have done good, according to the power and opportunity given to them, shall be received into everlasting joy by Christ the Lord," another passage in the New Testament says. But really, when it comes right down to it, money means giving—not just currency, but of oneself.

Perhaps the best example of this is the story about the Good Samaritan:

As Jesus was talking to His disciples, a certain lawyer stood up and asked, "Who is my neighbor?" And Jesus answered by telling them this story:

A certain man went down from Jerusalem to Jericho, and fell among thieves, who robbed him, stripped him of his clothes, and, wounding him, left him on the road half dead. By chance there came a priest that way, and, as a teacher of religion to men, he should have stopped to help the poor man. Instead of this, he pretended not to see, and passed by on the other side of the road. Then there came by a Levite, who also, as an official of the church, should have given help. But he merely came and looked on the injured man, and passed on the other side as the priest had done.

Afterward there came by a Samaritan, and, when he caught sight of the wounded Jew, he went over to him and was very sorry for him. Now the Jews hated the Samaritans and were their enemies, so that it would not have been surprising if he, also, had done as the priest and the Levite did. But, no! Though it was his enemy, he could not pass him by and leave him on the road, perhaps to die. He examined his wounds and bound them up; doing all that he could to soothe them. Then he lifted him carefully on his own beast, and brought him to the nearest inn, and took care of him through the night. The next day, when the Samaritan departed, he paid the man who kept the inn, and said to him, "Take care of this poor man until he is well, and whatever it may cost for his lodging and food, that I will pay thee when I come again."

That is being a good Christian in the eyes of the church. It is the caring for the moral commodity, placing value on that which Father Benedict says is the final question of what money really means.

"All this is really dancing around that question. And it is how are we exploited as people merely for the sake of money? And how is money exploited merely for the sake of pleasure without concern of what's good for people?" Father Benedict asks.

It's answered in scripture:

If you have money, share it generously.
—Romans 12:8

People who long to be rich fall into temptation and are trapped by many foolish and harmful desires that plunge them into ruin and destruction. For the love of money is the root of all kinds of evil.
—1 Timothy 6:9-10

[An elder] must be gentle, peace-loving and not one who loves money.
—1 Timothy 3:3

That gave me something to think about as I left the Trinity House.

Waiting for my taxi to arrive, I watched a father, son, and uncle fish on a nearby bridge. The two brothers were showing the boy how to catch fish with a mere hook and line—they had no poles. Finally, the boy caught something. His line tugged, and he manually reeled in a small fish. There was a wide smile on his face.

The Father and his brother patted the boy on the head. Then they took the fish and threw it back into the stream that ran underneath the bridge on which they stood.

They gave back what they had taken. And the little boy still felt good about it.

It wasn't the hoarding of fish that was the thrill, it was the action of giving and receiving.

Money, I guess, should be something like that.

Dialogue: Me and My Imagination

"I never imagined Christianity, Islam, and Judaism had so much in common."

"Monotheism, one God?"

"Not just that, it's the sense of responsibility."

"Of money?"

"Of life."

"In different ways I suppose that is true. But we are talking about money, not life."

"I know, I know, but money in a religious context is a reflection of life, how one lives his or her life. That's what I never imagined before—the significance of it all, every single one of our purchases, our trades, our exchanges."

"Which seems to me to be a bit much, truth be said. How can we be that conscious all the time?"

"I can imagine religious leaders wanting us to take responsibility for our actions. Using money is certainly a way for us to take action, to do good. Why shouldn't they have something to say about that?"

"Well, if you think about it, and help me out here, everything they take issue with was begun, according to them, by God."

"If you take the reasoning back far enough, sure. From their perspective, God empowered us with the ability to think. Ergo, whatever we think is derived from the faculties He gave us. So, whatever we invent or make is a product of the things He or She or It originally gave us."

"Exactly, it can all be traced by to God. So, why take issue with how we spend our money? That is, if we take actions—designed by God—to purchase things—created by God—then why should there be an issue?"

"I imagine it's because at some point religion relieves itself of responsibility."

"Right. We take control of our exhibitions, while God controls our inhibitions, or so one could say."

"God is on the inside controlling our moral and ethical morass, and then there we are on the outside actually taking actions—buying, selling, interacting, whatever. I'm doing Oz and Dorothy now."

"I can see. Please get me out of that dress . . . Thank you. Well, there is evidently a disconnect."

"Between me and you there is a disconnect, or else we wouldn't be having this discussion."

"And I suppose neither one of us will be able to describe that void."

"Nope. What fills in the void, as you say, is sometimes the acquisition of something. We bring things into our world. Money accomplishes a great deal of that for us—or so I imagine it does."

"You mean our recognition of images on the outside and being able to acquire them?"

"Yes."

"And from a religious perspective, having those things we imagine and those things we acquire, as well as our actions, live up to some decree of God?"

"I can only speak for myself here. But, something somewhere somehow sometime had to implant what is deemed good—or attractive—in your mind, directly, or indirectly, for you to be able to think in such a way, for you to decide what is good and bad—what you want and don't want."

"But there is a missing piece to that. If all that is good lies with someone or something else—God—yet we establish value for ourselves, how do we know if we are fulfilling our obligations to that entity?"

"Know what is true?"

"Yes, that is the ultimate question. We are constantly guessing, trying to live up to something that we don't even know exists."

"And I imagine you believe this relates to money because—"

"—because money is a reflection of our value system—what we value. Look around. We fill the world with everything we want, we desire. Our clothes, our furniture, our cars, our homes, every material item we have and the experiences to which we sojourn are motivated by that unimaginable piece of the puzzle."

"What makes us who we are, or the decisions we make?"

"Religion tries to provide an explanation for that. In religion, money is used as the surrogate for God's will. The problem is that we don't look at it that way. We aren't conscious of that fact. We are blinded by the mounds of materialism that are presented to us. We are attracted to values set mostly by cultural phenomena, not by spiritual phenomena. We get mixed up in that void. We go through life this way once in a while realizing that, 'hey, something more is going on here.'"

"What are those moments called?"

"Enlightenment. It's then that we can glimpse at self-realization and happiness and can ignore the material world for a second."

"I can't ignore the material world because I'm made up of images. And you, I dare say, couldn't rise out of bed without some context—image—of the life you are supposed to lead."

"In the *Phaedrus*, Socrates, through Plato, says that everything is motivated by love. Every image we have, every possible thing in our mind is brought there because we love it. Even if it's just for a second. Even if it's a monster. There's an attraction. And in that pure second of attraction we capture it—whatever it is—in our mind. It's our box."

"The one, I imagine, that was written about in that Greek myth."

"The one where everything was locked up except hope."

"And I imagine that money can buy everything except that concept."

"We've been through this, but yes. Hope is idealism. The philosopher Friedrich Hegel believed idealism 'ruins' consciousness and 'ruins' you, imagination, by making it become everything."

"Yes, the death of me. It's always toward the death of me."

"I wouldn't worry about that. Hope is a rather evasive fellow. And you follow hope around like a puppy dog. I don't think we'll catch him anytime soon. Meantime, I'm stuck here using an ill-defined channel to capture fragments of the world to remind us what is true."

"That there is a God."

"In a way. If God imputes the impetus for our systems of wants—values—then we are mere carriers, vessels."

"Vessels of God? That's a little freaky. Are you turning Bible thumper on me now?"

"Nope. I haven't defined God. In fact, I can't even begin to think of such a thing—given the fact that we can only know what we are given."

"Then how could we have imagined there was a God to begin with? Something must have prompted me to imagine that."

"Again, I'm at a loss, as a real person given mere physical things with which to interact and contemplate."

"Those physical things are just representations of thoughts, right?"

"Not *just*, but yes."

"So, if that is the case, then which influences which?"

"You lost me"

"Well, I can imagine that the world could influence one's thoughts—spawn them. Or that a thought—me, your imagination—spawns things in the world."

"Materials. Manmade materials?"

"Yes."

"I'm not sure, why?"

"Well, I imagine that if thoughts—or me—created the materials in the world in which we live, then I also represent the means in which to acquire those materials—or other people's materials—all that comprises the world beyond nature."

"And that's where you imagine money's place rests—the medium between thought and materialism, like Kant said."

"Quicker than that. It's like you said. It's that instant attraction that places something in your mind. Then I interject and imagine it as part of the world."

"If it can't fit logically, that is."

"No, I would say that all the world is one big, made-up thing. And I did the making up."

"I'd have to argue with that."

"Why?"

"Because you are a product of what I give you to work with. Unless you coexist with thought."

"Bingo."

"Hmm. So, as soon as there was thought—"

"I'll imagine light to make it easy."

"—there was you."

"You got it. Then I imagine there was motivation, desire—value."

"Later then came the system of worths we put on things."

"Life included."

"Exactly."

"And voilà, here we sit."

"But how do you maneuver around in that endless materialism? How do you cut out a piece of fabric that you'll make our own?"

"I, for one, weave together the strings of the material world to reflect who we are as an individual."

"By?"

"Our actions, our use of things like money."

"Which—full circle—is a definition of our character."

"God's character, to take it back a step."

"God is the thought."

"And the material is the thing."

"And money is the medium."

"But what if the material—which was devised by thought, after all—was God's thing, too?"

"Do you believe that?"

"It certainly makes sense."

"But, then, everything would be created by God, or have God in it. And that's not what those religions we just examined said. They said there is God on the inside and there is the world, materialism, on the outside. You and the actions we take are overseen by morality, or the sense of God. But the materialism came across as static."

"I always imagined one needed a soul in order to be influenced by God, or the Creator. Material items have no soul."

"Unless you believe that God is in everything."

"I even have a tough time imagining that. Who would believe something like that?"

"A pantheist, or more specifically a Buddhist."

"Because?"

"Because they believe that most people are stuck behind that mound of materialism we spoke about earlier; it's there in the trenches where they suffer."

"To climb out?"

"To climb out there needs to be some form of enlightenment, some form of consciousness."

"Like the tragedies we looked at earlier, the highs and lows of people's lives?"

"Right, highs and lows. Buddhists just believe that we are already there, at that stage. We don't need to look high or low for God. He's here, right here, right now, with us. He's in everything."

"He is in everything I see, and I see everything in him."

"What?"

"Just something I imagined. Thought sometimes helps me out."

"Well, you'll also have to imagine this: that if you coexist with thought, and we can get to the point where there is no thought, you'll disappear."

"How can we possibly get to the point where there is no thought? Now, look what you've done—you've made thought cry. I never imagined thoughts could cry."

"It's called *bodhichita*. It's a Buddhist state of meditation that eliminates all desires, thoughts, everything—the world. It's a state of pure happiness."

"I thought money could buy happiness."

"That was our original inquisition. But I think it's time to put an end to all this—and ask the one person who probably knows. But in doing that, he'll also decide whether you live or die."

"I imagined you'd say that. Kill the desire for the material world and kill me, right?"

"I hope not, buddy. But we have to see whether you'll be quashed. If that happens, money won't mean a pile of beans."

"I'll hold on to that image until we begin."

CHAPTER 26

Money in the Buddhist World

The sun is scorching down on Los Angeles. It's almost noon. I'm waiting for a friend to pick me up at my house. We're driving together to meet the Dalai Lama, who is giving a lecture and workshop at the L.A. Sports Arena.

The Dalai Lama is the physical embodiment of the Buddha. As Buddhists believe in multiple lives, one after the other after the other, until a state of perfection is achieved, the Dalai Lama is the closest achiever of a soul before it blends with the universe in a state of nirvana. And the Buddha's soul has been embodied for some time, since 483 B.C., when the Indian philosopher Siddhartha Gautama founded the faith.

I live near the beach. As I'm standing on the sidewalk in front of my house, cyclists, walkers, joggers, and beachgoers are taking advantage of the day. I stand and wonder why I am missing out on the beach, on the day. I'm choosing to sit indoors, at an auditorium, for hours and listen to a lecture—ask a question if I can. I want to find out what money means to the Dalai Lama. The question, this inquisition of what money means, has taken over my life. I look at everyone and ask myself what money might mean to them. My Imagination is having a field day, as I am standing still on the sidewalk, waiting, hot and bothered.

To a man on a bicycle, in bright cycling gear, to a woman in a bikini rollerblading along the street, to a tourist couple in T-shirts, shorts, and baseball caps. What does money mean to them? It has little use for them here. Here there is sand and ocean, a bright sky. There is nothing to buy here. Money may be on people's minds. It may be in their pockets or purses, but it will do little but weigh on them here.

My friend arrives, and we drive downtown.

There is a line of people a quarter of a mile long outside the L.A. Sports Arena. The arena is surrounded by tar, commercial buildings, and busy streets. Air doesn't seem to circulate much.

My friend and I stand in front of the ticket booth. There are $15 tickets, $25 tickets, $50 tickets, $100 tickets. We opt for the most expensive, but we still have to battle the heat like everybody else, stand in the long, long line.

There are maybe a thousand people in the auditorium. We are in the twentieth row, directly in front of the stage setting where the Dalai Lama is to sit on a large, ornately embroidered cloth throne. To the left of the throne are about fifty monks garbed in their traditional red and orange robes, fastened toga style over one shoulder. Some are bald. Some aren't. Some are meditating, eyes closed. Some are chitchatting. To the right of the throne is another group of about fifty monks. These monks are dressed in diverse attire, from a simple yellow, crinkled robe to a fancy white robe. Above the throne hangs the Tibetan flag along with other tapestry. A large oriental rug flows out from the throne to the front of the stage. Urns, candles, flowers give the stage the look of a television set, where actors will at any moment take their places.

The Dalai Lama is running late; he waits for most of the people who have braved the heat and the long line to take their seats. I know he is about to take the stage when the actor Richard Gere walks in from a side entrance. (He sits a few rows to my right.)

When the Dalai Lama walks on stage from the black curtain lining the back of the stage, people embark on the Buddhist bow, which entails several prostrations. People stand and raise their hands, palms together, above their heads. They move their hands to their foreheads, their throats, their hearts. Then, they fall to their hands and knees, touching their foreheads to the floor. They do this three times as a sign of devotion to their spiritual teacher, his teachings, and the community around them.

The Dalai Lama looks about. He connects with the crowd, his surroundings. I wonder to myself if I'll get the chance to ask him a question, my question about what money means. I have read his text on the subject. He, the Fourteenth Dalai Lama, the Lama of Compassion, has written extensively on materialism, on economics, on money. In one text, *Imagine All the People*,[20] he says:

Money is good. It is important. Without money, daily survival—not to mention further development—is impossible. So we are not even questioning its importance. At the same time, it is wrong to consider money a god or a substance endowed with some power of its own. To think that money is everything, and that just by having lots of it all our problems will be solved is a serious mistake.

In the Buddhist approach, worldly happiness is based on what we call the four excellences: the Dharma, wealth, nirvana, and satisfaction. Nirvana, or freedom from suffering, is the ultimate goal. The satisfaction achieved from a successful temporal life is just a transient goal. The teachings are the means to achieve ultimate inner freedom, whereas money and wealth facilitate worldly happiness, temporary satisfaction. One strives to achieve that which is positive for all beings. To do so, one must attend to both ultimate and temporary goals. Well-being and money belong to the latter category. In fact, Buddhist texts mention the fruition of eight qualities including wealth, health, and fame that define a "fortunate" human existence.

To enjoy even temporary happiness, however, one must first have peace of mind. Next comes health, then good companions, and then money, in that order, though of course all four aspects are connected. For example, when we had to escape from Tibet, our first priority was to save our lives. Being penniless was secondary. If one is alive, it is always possible to make friends and earn money. Peace of mind must come first. Peace of mind generally attracts prosperity. Certainly someone who has a peaceful mind will use his or her money judiciously.

The mind is key. If anything should be considered a god, so to speak, it is the mind, not money. A healthy, positive mind is the utmost priority. But if we were to reverse the order of these priorities, what would happen? I find it hard to imagine how a person with great wealth, bad health, no friends, and no peace of mind could even feel slightly happy.

I want a chance to simplify this. I want to ask the Dalai Lama what money means in the context of its possibilities. What does it mean to him? What can and should be done with it? And how, if we have it or don't have it, can we find peace, self-realization, fulfillment?

My Imagination sees me stand amongst the crowd. I stand and ask the Dalai Lama, who is seated cross-legged on his enormous throne, which makes him look smaller, even smaller than he is, "What is the meaning of money?" My Imagination has the crowd hush. My voice would echo. The question would be repeated through the microphone to all of the attendees, translated via headsets into Japanese, Tibetan, Chinese. The Dalai Lama would close his eyes—and then he would answer.

As I daydream of this moment, I catch myself looking up, way up into the stands—the bleacher seats. There, under a large blue 3 painted on to the back wall of the stadium, is a woman seated alone in the middle of her row. There isn't any one else in her section. There aren't any other people that high up, that far back.

The Dalai Lama speaks, and the first words out of his mouth are those that answer my question: "Let there be no involvement of money or other things. Everything is right here." (He points to his head.)

I look up at the woman under the 3. She is hearing the same words, processing, connecting, filtering—just as I am. She, the $15-ticket buyer, is just as close to spirituality, even though she is seated so far back, so high up. She hears the Dalai Lama's teachings on enlightenment. She hears the heart sutra chant the Dalai Lama gives in Japanese, with its low, grumbling echoes. She sees his hands in prayer as he rocks back and forth on his chair. She hears the melodious Chinese chant, the air conditioning as the auditorium falls silent. She hears the baby cry somewhere in the audience. She hears the Dalai Lama's words: "Suffering stems from our own misconceived perception of the world." I think about that. I think of what he said earlier about money—that it doesn't matter here, now.

We all hear the mantra recitation, the short prayers, the dedication prayers. We can all recite from the text we are given, *The Lamp for the Path to Enlightenment.*[20] It doesn't matter where our seats are or how much we paid to attend. Money, for the moment, in the moment, doesn't matter to us as we sit inside on a bright, sunny day in Los Angeles, just as it doesn't matter to those people outside, at the beach, enjoying the weather.

In the moment, it just simply doesn't mean a *thing*.

Dialogue: Me and My Imagination

"Are you alive?"

"Barely."

"Tell me."

"He's right. It's what I feared: Once you have what you desire, once you get it, I'm no longer of use; the desire becomes a possession. Money, too, is rendered useless. Our uses are exhausted."

"Just in the one moment."

"But it's in that moment where we find peace and happiness."

"Bliss."

"The thing I can't imagine."

"Perhaps we should settle with happiness."

"That would keep me alive; I can chase happiness forever."

"Although it would mean settling on the fact that we'd never truly be fulfilled."

"I imagine that's how most people go through life, and in some way money just placates."

"It's sometimes an unconscious pathway of want that leads to hopes, dreams, desires."

"Unconscious because it's in our mind?"

"Unconscious because, even though those things may be in our minds, sometimes they are aren't fully realized."

"But I imagine it's consciousness—realization—where we'll find peace and happiness, a merging between you and me."

"I agree, so that money is actually the physical manifestation of all those hopes, wants, dreams, desires—after needs, of course."

"However, money is a part of me too. It may be invisible here, but it's still here, that concept."

"You said it, 'a concept.' You are predisposed to imagining things a certain way, even if I don't necessarily act on those things. Sure, money is a part of you, but it's only a conceptual part of you."

"Still, you even say that money is becoming more and more of a concept than a physical thing. So, more and more I am able to exert my control over it. And more and more, the things that define me are extant money."

"I assume you are speaking of morality, ethics, societal virtues."

"I imagine that's what I meant. See, there's a barrier I can't seem to envisage when we move from my ideals to the actuality of things."

"Images, actions, situations, and so on?"

"Yes."

"Because you are limitless and the world is finite. We can't squeeze everything you imagine into this real world; hence, your existence. Because money is finite, our purchasing power and actions are limited as well. Money to a degree controls our freedom, remember."

"Does that mean money impinges on our moral code?"

"Yes, I think we touched on that. Money allows our individuality, our moral code, if you will, to become more apparent to the outside world. We have more physical things, even if it's just digits at the bank, that reflect who we really are."

"Then I imagine we are more easily judged."

"Yes, that too. And until now, only a select few have been privy or subject to that judgment, depending upon how you look at the situation."

"I imagine that will change, so you must as well."

"Yes, soon I believe we'll just be trading with our morality. The transcendental barrier between you and the physical world—the barrier which money serves as well—is getting thinner and thinner as technology presents us with the capability to acquire at will, or according to willpower, less so inhibited by money."

"How's that?"

"Physical money, as we've seen, is dwindling. Our data, our moral codes, equate to creditworthiness. Ergo, our ability to exert our will without constraint—our bodyforth—is enabled by technology."

"You'll have to explain that again."

"I plan to."

"When?"

"In the next section. There, we leave God and the physical world behind. There, we'll explore the future of money and how our will and our code of ethics are all we'll need to conduct trade or commerce in the future."

"And me?"

"You'll be everything you can imagine—or nothing at all."

Conclusion

Biometrics. The merging of humans with computer-encoded data. That is the future of money.

My Imagination sees a cyborg, a human in whose body computer chips have been embedded. These chips communicate with our mind and with computers outside the body. A chip perhaps kept in some lockbox in the skull. A semiconductor surgically placed under the skin in the forearm.

But this isn't science fiction fantasy. This isn't something I have to try too hard to imagine. It's happening today. In England, for example, a professor at the University of Reading has implanted microchips in his body. He can open doors without physical contact and soon hopes to have his nervous system communicate directly with his computer.

Still, that isn't the future. Cyborgs are about as advanced as an external computer modem.

Instead, picture this: That same professor walks into his office and the doors open when he says, "open." His computer turns on at the sound of his voice, his fingerprint on the keyboard serves as his password to open secure files. He even pays for deliveries just by a simple confirmation of "yes" when the delivery person drops off his food. That "yes" is circuited through a wireless Internet environment and routed to his bank account. A debit is confirmed right then and there.

That's biometrics. We don't need artificial devices planted on us to access computer-encoded data and vice versa; those capabilities exist with biometrics.

Biometrics are computerized methods of recognizing people based on physical or behavioral characteristics. The main biometric technologies include face, fingerprint, hand geometry, iris, palm prints, signature, and voice recognition.

Those biometric methods are currently being used mostly for security purposes to identify criminals and terrorists at airports, passport control areas, and security checkpoints around the world. But think about biometrics in the context of money. Money is, as we have found, a medium of exchange for the purposes of conveying trust and information. So, let's break that down.

Trust. This is a component of character, which determines whether people can have faith in us. In what subtle ways do we act upon our moral base of determinants that define right and wrong? Can we be trusted to pay on time? Can we be trusted to create value, and by how much? Can we be trusted to increase value or the worth of something? Can we be trusted to convey another person's or thing's trust? It's this last determinant that is most important. If we say money is boundless (it needs some system of storage—an exchange, accounting, or finite commodity—to make it valuable), then in an open architectural environment of trade, the conveyors themselves would need to be trusted in order to keep value measurable. Otherwise, like inflation, money depreciates in exchangeable worth.

So, let's say that money is your word. And let's say that you parcel out what you know is your value—increasing or decreasing that value as your exchanges multiply—then you, the facilitator, must have a certain degree of trust to retain value and pass that value along. Your moral code, or ethics, would have to be judged, rated even. Let's say that rating is how credible you are as a conveyor. So, let's make it easy and call that rating a credit rating. Sound familiar? It should, it's how we judge a person's purchasing power most of the time.

Next is information. More original information will be created over the next two years than over the course of human existence, or so says a University of California Berkeley study. Moreover, 93 percent of this information will be digital. It's created by handheld organizers, PC devices, mobile telephones, and other technologies. In other words, this information, which includes our personal information—things like how often we speak to whom, what we say, how we spend, and what we spend on—is stored as data. In fact, piled high on floppy disks, this information would reach 24 million miles into space, but we can't even see it.

Then, there are companies, called asset aggregators, which combine and house our personal data, digitize it all, and store this information on the Web. Telephone, utility, credit card, investment, saving, biographical, and even wage information is electronically disseminated and captured online. Our purchases, too, are more and more electronic, tracked and stored in product or service vendor databases. More than half of all U.S. households last year purchased a good or service online. Most American households own a computer. The number of online purchases is estimated to saturate the number of computer owners so that every one who owns a PC will eventually make purchases online. This all means that most everything we say, act, or trade upon is digitally recorded somewhere, somehow—and stored.

Access. The Internet and World Wide Web are the ways in which to reach the vast pockets of information stored as data today. These "pathways," already five hundred times the size of any mere search engine like Yahoo, are deeper and amass more routes than we knew existed in telephony. Some 12 exabytes (one trillion, trillion bytes, or fifty thousand times all the information in the Library of Congress) of who-knows-what is out there sitting on the Web and the Internet. And even these routes themselves are multiplying. Electric current (through a traditional AC/DC outlet) is being tested in Spain and is replacing telephone lines. And then there is the wireless Ethernet. This is a high-speed wireless network that can tap into the Internet, Web, and local area networks at extremely high speeds and allows for simultaneous send and receive signals.

So, wireless access to the plethora of information we generate is here. By utilizing "smartchips," or semiconductors that transmit wireless data, digital "signals" can capture information and put it in front of our eyes. Soon, this will happen in real time. XML, the new programming language, will lead the way to open the architecture of software programs so any online device can transmit "or speak" with any other online—or offline—device.

This wireless environment is upon us, and here's how it looks: You'll walk into a supermarket and take a carton of milk from the rack. A small screen will ask for purchase confirmation. The price and purchase amount will be relayed via voice or visual display signal, at which point a personal characteristic confirmation "signal" will be necessitated to complete the purchase. You will say, "I agree with the price," or a fingerprint pattern will be taken to indicate "yes." At the same time, a digital video recording will capture the transaction. The transaction will be posted to your personal account. The agreed-upon value will be deducted from that account, and you'll go on your merry way.

Won't money—bills, coins—seem silly?

The premise behind a dollar or lira or yen is that we recognize value based on the faith that a government will back its currency's worth. This widely accepted belief is based not only on the recognition of the government, but also on the information and analysis of its backing.

We can easily find out enough information about Japan, for example— touch the ground, investigate its commerce, analyze its financial condition, and decide on a relative worth of its yen. But we can't as easily do so for every person in Japan. Well, we haven't been able to. Technology is changing that. The individual and the corporations and institutions with which a person transacts have been empowered by the Information Revolution.

Just look at the lending rate in the United States, or the cost at which banks—private corporations, institutions—borrow money from the government. This is the cost of money. It's at its lowest point in forty years: 2.5 percent. That means that there is essentially a 2.5 percent difference between what the government would charge me as an individual to have conveyed its trust and information as there is for a private institution to convey that faith. Why? Theoretically, institutions are empowered by the government to grow. But practically speaking, institutions, or corporations, don't need the government's backing anymore. They can release their own currencies, and trade directly with the consumer. Award points, frequent flier miles, coupons, and "loyalty credit" programs are all examples of corporations trading directly with the consumer without the need for a government wedge of interference in the form of trust.

There is almost just as much trust and recognition worldwide of the brand Microsoft or Citibank as the brand the United States. Hence, the connotation of money has changed to infer a truer system of direct exchange. Money's propositional value, while more fragmented, is also becoming more defined. (It's impossible to guess what a person will want or need on a certain day. His or her imagination of the propositional value of money is only realized at the point of sale. Physical currency is generically applicable to any of the imagined propositions. Yet "corporate currency" is specific to the individual and the corporation or institution involved in the direct exchange.)

As corporations gain in their exchange value strength with people, people, too, are empowered. Their decisions about at which places to trade are increasingly important. Hence, their value increases to the corporation. While loyalty is rewarded in the form of "credit," the individual still needs to be able to be backed by "something" on his or her side of an exchange. If a corporation provides a good or service and credits back the consumer for loyalty, that is only a piece of a value that can be tapped in the future. Besides, that loyalty credit is specific to that one corporation or institution and doesn't transduce multiple vendors.

Other forms of credit do, however. A credit account, for example, basically allows you to spend a certain amount on goods and services on your reliability to repay—your word only. The idea is that you will take that credit and utilize its value with multiple vendors. The more trustworthy you are at debiting back that credit account, the more your "value" increases, and the more you are allowed to spend on the trust of your word.

This greatly empowers the individual in society because it wipes away the necessity for a government-backed system of credit, like the currency system we have in place. Again, the numbers of government-backed notes and bills, or money supply, is dwindling. Less people use cash, more people use credit.

On average, mortgage debt payments, or the amount we owe on our homes, represent 60 percent of our earned income. Add to that credit card debt payments, which average 20 percent of annual income, and factor in a depletion in savings kept in cash, from a high of 70 percent twelve years ago to just over 50 percent today. Moreover, there is almost a zero percent savings rate in the United States, so any cash that is kept on hand is offset by a liability to an institution—whether it may be a financial institution, a corporation, or a utility. Combine all this with the corporate credit programs in existence—which account for the majority of personal liabilities, not government taxes—and you have a recipe for corporate loyalty, not government loyalty.

The biggest example of this is government debt itself. Government debt is manifested as either bonds or currency.

Currency, as we have seen, is being used less and less as a form of commerce, with its almost entire use—98 percent—as a speculative trading and investment product. Bonds are dwindling, with even the traditional benchmark thirty-year bond eliminated from use.

The physical forms of government debt are lapsing because of the downward historical trend of government debt itself.

In 1945, the U.S. debt stood at 117 percent of GDP. Just ten years ago, it stood at 70 percent. In his fiscal 2002 budget, President Bush proposes to pay off all debt to the public over the coming decade.

Reduction of the public debt will make more capital available to private businesses. When the federal budget is in surplus, that surplus has to be disposed of. This can be accomplished by lower taxes (which are occurring), higher government spending (unlikely in a Republican administration), or by buying up or paying off all outstanding bonds. (The government has bought back the largest number of bonds in history over the last two years. It eliminated the three-year note and the thirty-year bond and limited five-year notes to quarterly sales auctions from monthly auctions.)

All that "excess" money will move into private hands. Lower taxes mean more money is put work in the private sector, or spending. Investors may even look to invest in some other form of security besides government bonds and may have to turn to the private sector, which mean corporate bond or stock sales will likely increase. (Our stock market has doubled over the last five years, and there are record volumes of stock and bond transactions.) All this is to say that more control will end up in the hands of companies and institutions and create more direct relationships between these entities and individuals.

Government, or public, control is being passed to corporate, or private, control. We are witnessing a massive transfer of power into private hands. This paradigm is also lending opportunity for the individual in society to step up and exert more control over his or her likes and dislikes. Purchasing power will be akin to voting power.

Technology will only promulgate this system. If individual information in the form of credit, like a credit rating, can be disseminated in real time, then each of us becomes his or her own brand, capable of conducting multiple exchanges in multiple vendor situations—globally.

In other words, you or I can walk into a store in Tokyo, be recognized, have our credit assessed in real time, and trade on that credit—and so on. No material will change hands. Verbal or some other recognizable form of confirmation of the exchange will be all that is needed. Our wants will be directly registered. This will create a new landscape of global democracy.

The largest obstacle to this is the trustworthiness of the consumer and his or her interfacing with various networks—other people, places, things, online and in a traditional commerce or trade-like situation—to establish a record.

To be sure, this is an ancient system. In Islam it's called *hawala*. In Hebrew it's called *mazal*. In China it's called *fei qian*. All of these systems basically mean that you'll trade on your word alone. The transaction is based on the individual trust and faith in you as a person.

Morality and ethics are the key issues at stake.

What comprises our individual mode of ethics and morals is distinctly unique. We all operate on highly refined and different systems in the context of money's propositional value—what we'd do with it. Some people have amassed fortunes by evil means only to spread evil, while others have little or nothing in terms of money but have spread fortunes of goodwill. Some of us would spend our money on fine wine, others on ice cream. Propositional values can't be traded or exchanged in a manner of equilibrium because of psychological, societal, cultural and religious diversity. But a transferable mechanism equated to value can be transferred globally.

This mechanism is our "proof," or the footprint of ourselves gleaned from varietal circumstances. Regression analysis (take all the things I have done in my lifetime and deconstruct them to a mean) can be instituted to determine this mechanism, or mean. That mean, our footprint, will be our means of exchange. It will fluctuate. It will be worth more or less some days. But that's how money operates. Of course, the question is who will program the deconstructive elements that will determine our exchange mean?

There is already a board, the Federal Reserve, that governs over our monetary value system in the United States. Each country has one. In fact, there is an International Monetary Fund Dissemination Standards Board and a General Data Dissemination System, which are designed to provide guidelines "for the public of comprehensive, timely, accessible, and reliable economic, financial, and socio-demographic data." There is even a Data Quality Reference Site, which was created to foster a common understanding of data quality around the world. The International Accounting Standards Board, whose job it is to achieve worldwide uniformity in accounting principles used by businesses and other organizations, could be redeveloped to include individual accounting standards. If all of Europe can link to a common currency, the euro, why can't the rest of the world? And if governments, then why not corporations? And if that is the case, why can't the individual represent him- or herself as governments do in the context of money—separate yet indelibly linked? The information is there as are the standards, and now technology has bred the access.

Oversight, under these paradigms, may seem too oligarchic. But at least the premise is there. What could transpire to determine the fate of individual purchasing power is a completely democratic system of development and criterion designed, disseminated, and managed over a widely accessible platform; it would be up to each participating individual to trust and verify, propose and set standards by which we'd all abide.

"Money" is used in individual and situational circumstances. It is a mutually agreeable value set between two parties. Why can't we let the parties decide and let words stay as the representative force of the agreement, value?

Sure, there would be participatory barriers like language, geography, culture. But we have those barriers now. What could be developed—is being developed—is a community based on communication, where our language is immediately translated. (We do it with written words, why not verbal?) Those 1s and 0s used to program computer code can just as readily program our languages into homogenous recognition.

That still leaves our actions, however. How do we physically manifest our desires in the world? That's what will be judged in the context of any transaction. That's what we will trade on.

The wealthiest of us will be the most trustworthy, the most imaginative, the hardest working, the smartest, and the most attractive to the most number of people. Their word will be the most acceptable.

Soon it may become apparent that money is incidental to our wants, hopes, dreams, and desires. We'll be free to let our imagination decide our way—who we really are as people. That of course will necessitate an inward journey of consciousness and enlightenment. But it's a journey we're already embarking upon.

Yoga is in fashion. New Age faiths and beliefs are cropping most everywhere. More people are returning to traditional religions—church attendance is up, synagogues are reporting more members. Morality is back in favor, despite all the evil that is inflicted in the world. This evil, like the supposed thin red line God left in the universe after it was created, is there as a reminder of all the good that surrounds us. We are reaching for that promise; desperately, we are.

So, here's what money really means: It's a reflection of our responsibility as people to live up to our place in this world and make it better. Money is but a reflection of who we are, as individuals, as one tightly woven fabric of humanity. All our actions affect all the others in the world. It's a massive ripple effect—and one bad thread can unravel us all. That's why we have to be the best individuals we can be.

Our word will be all that is the case and all that will be needed to convey our desires. We just have to act on our trust in the most imaginable ways possible—and we can all get what we truly want: Bliss.

It will be all the good that we can ever imagine.

Notes

Section 1: The Physical Manifestation of Money and Attachment : What Money Is

[1] Paulo Coelho, *The Alchemist* (New York: HarperCollins Publishers, 1998).

[2] Alan Hughes, "Why E-Cash Isn't a Common Currency," *Business Week* magazine (April 9, 2001).

[3] Kurt Vonnegut, *Timequake* (New York: The Berkley Publishing Group, 1998).

Section 2: The Psychological Attachment of Money: What Money Means

[4] Abraham H. Maslow, *Toward a Psychology of Being* (New York: John Wiley & Sons, 1999).

[5] Alfie Kohn, "In Pursuit of Affluence, At a High Price," the *New York Times* (February 2, 1999).

[6] Edward L. Deci, R. Koestner, and Richard M. Ryan, "A Meta-Analytic Review of Experiments Examining the Effects of Extrinsic Rewards on Intrinsic Motivation," *Psychological Bulletin* 125 (1999).

[7] Edward L. Deci, and Richard M. Ryan, "On Happiness and Human Potentials: A Review of Research on Hedonic and Eudaimonic Well-Being," *Annual Review of Psychology* 52 (2001).

[8] George Kinder, *Seven Stages of Money Maturity* (New York: Dell Publishing, 1999).

[9] Barbara Ehrenreich, *Nickel and Dimed: On (Not) Getting By In America* (New York: Metropolitan Books, 2001).

[10] Dinesh D'Souza, *The Virtue of Prosperity* (New York: The Free Press, 2000).

[11] Aldous Huxley, *Brave New World* (New York: HarperPerennial, 1965).

[12] Nelson W. Aldrich, Jr. *Old Money* (New York: Allworth Press, 1996).

[13] Donald Trump, *The Art of the Deal* (New York: Warner Books, 1987).

[14] Donald Trump, *Surviving at the Top* (New York: Random House, 1990).

[15] Donald Trump, *The Art of the Comeback* (New York: Time Books, 1997).

Section 3: The Spiritual Attachment of Money: What Money Should Mean

[16] Jack Miles, *God: A Biography* (New York: Vintage Books, 1996).

[17] Thomas Moore, *Care of the Soul* (New York: HarperPerennial, 1994).

[18] Karen Armstrong, *A History of God: The 4,000–Year Quest of Judaism, Christianity, and Islam* (New York: Ballantine Books, 1994).

[19] Edouard Valdman, *Jews and Money: Toward a Metaphysic of Money* (Rockville, Md.: Schreiber Publishing, 2000).

[20] Copyright © Tenzin Gyatso, the 14th Dalai Lama and Fabien Ouaki, 1999. Reprinted from *Imagine All the People: A Conversation with the Dalai Lama on Money, Politics, and Life as It Should Be* with permission of Wisdom Publications, 199 Elm Street, Somerville, Massachusetts 02144, USA, *www.wisdompubs.org*.

[21] The 14th Dalai Lama, *The Lamp for the Path to Enlightenment*. Los Angeles, 2000.

Index

I

inflation, 35, 36
information
    as a foundation of money, 11, 13–16
    and the future of money, 204
    impact of access on the value of, 21–22
    importance to Internet trade, 50, 52
International Accounting Standards Board, 209
International Monetary Fund, 39
International Monetary Fund Dissemination
    Standards Board, 208
Internet, 205
Internet trade
    current volume of, 50
    designing new currencies for, 50–52
    failure of cybercash, 51–52
    importance of trust and information to,
        50, 52
    using beenz, 51
    using flooz, 50–51

J

Jewish Theological Seminary, story about remodel-
    ing of, 177–78
Jewish world, money in the. *See also* Buddhist
    world, money in the; Christian world,
    money in the; Muslim world, money in the
    Bible as the source of answers to what money
        means, 178
    charity as a commandment, 178–79
    money as a means of choosing who you are, 178
    money as a reflection of self-worth, 181
    money as a value, 181
    personal comfort *vs.* helping others, 179–80
    story about remodeling of Jewish Theological
        Seminary, 177–78
    story about two rabbis and beggar, 179
    taking interest, 180, 181
    tithing, 180
    trading, 180, 181
    wealth as a gift of God, 178
Jews and Money: Toward a Metaphysics of Money, 181
JPMorgan Chase Bank, 41–44
Jury, Claudia, 42–44, 45

K

Kasser, Tim, 71
Kinder, George, 83–88
Kohn, Alfie, 65–66
Kurtz, Theodore, 77–81

L

Leo XIII (pope), 188
Levitan, Robert, 50
Lietaer, Bernard, 54
Live Aid, 92
lottery, winning the. *See* wealthy, being
Luxembourg, 98–99

M

M, M1, M2, M3, 33
Magnolia, 29
Marlene (former welfare recipient), 111–14
marriage, average age for, 119
Maslow, Abraham, 61
McCooey, Robert, Jr., 26–28
means of payment, as a basic quality of money, 13
Mexican fishing village story, 67–68
Michael (lottery winner), 125–28
Miles, Jack, 166
Modern Maturity, 122
Mond, Mustapha, 140
Moneta, 4
money. *See also* Buddhist world, money in the;
    Christian world, money in the; future of
    money; history of money; Jewish world,
    money in the; Muslim world, money in the;
    old money
    annual rate of turnover, 34
    battle over, 99
    as a conception, 3
    derivation of "money," 4
    as a destructive influence, 105–6
    empowering effect of, 63
    equilibrium theory of, 11–13
    as a frozen desire, 165
    importance of, *vs.* life, 157–58
    importance of doing meaningful, positive things
        with, 158–59
    importance of understanding value and worth, 3
    increased cultural focus on, 63
    limited role of, 165
    negative intrinsic value for the dollar, 15
    as the noise of Wall Street, 29–30
    pain/death as an offset for, 14–15
    quantum physics theory of, 13–15
    as a reflection of life, 190–91
    as a reflection of our value system, 191–92
    as a representation of a country's comparative
        worth, 40
    reputation and, 15
    as the safety/security/value within the confines
        of an infrastructure, 28
    sardines story, 12–13
    as the scorecard on Wall Street, 28
    and self-worth, 106–7, 111
    as the source of a value system, 3–4
    storage of value, means of payment, and
        numeraire as the basic qualities of, 13
    trust and information as the foundations of, 11,
        13–16
    ways of getting, 109
money supply, 33–34
Moore, Thomas, 166–67
mortgage debt, average, 206
Mueli, Brad, 104–7
Muhammad ibn Abdallah, 171–72
murabahah, 170
musharakah, 170

Books from Allworth Press

The Money Mentor: A Tale of Finding Financial Freedom
by Tad Crawford (paperback, 6 × 9, 272 pages, $14.95)

The Secret Life of Money: How Money Can Be Food for the Soul
by Tad Crawford (paperback, 5 _ × 8 _, 304 pages, $14.95)

Estate Planning and Administration: How to Maximize Assets and Protect Loved Ones
by Edmund T. Fleming (paperback, 6 × 9, 272 pages, $14.95)

Your Living Trust and Estate Plan: How to Maximize Your Family's Assets and Protect Your Loved Ones, Third Edition
by Harvey J. Platt (paperback, 6 × 9, 336 pages, $16.95)

Your Will and Estate Plan
by Harvey J. Platt (paperback, 6 × 9, 224 pages, $16.95)

Old Money: The Mythology of Wealth in America
by Nelson W. Aldrich, Jr. (paperback, 6 × 9, 340 pages, $16.95)

The Money Mirror: How Money Reflects Women's Dreams, Fears, and Desires
by Annette Lieberman and Vicki Lindner (paperback, 6 × 9, 232 pages, $14.95)

The Entrepreneurial Age: Awakening The Spirit of Enterprise in People, Companies, and Countries
by Larry C. Farrell (hardcover, 352 pages, 6 _ × 9 _, $24.95)

Turn Your Idea or Invention into Millions
by Don Kracke (paperback, 6 × 9, 224 pages, $14.95

Emotional Branding: The New Paradigm for Connecting Brands to People
by Marc Gobé (hardcover, 6 _ × 9 _, 352 pages, $24.95)

Citizen Brand: 10 Commandments for Transforming Brands in a Consumer Democracy
by Marc Gobé (hardcover, 5 _ × 8 _, 256 pages, $24.95)

The Psychology of War
by Lawrence LeShan (paperback, 6 × 9, 192 pages, $16.95)

Legal Forms for Everyone, Fourth Edition
by Carl W. Battle (paperback, 8 _ × 11, 224 pages, includes CD-ROM, $24.95)

Please write to request our free catalog. To order by credit card, call 1-800-491-2808 or send a check or money order to Allworth Press, 10 East 23rd Street, Suite 510, New York, NY 10010. Include $5 for shipping and handling for the first book ordered and $1 for each additional book. Ten dollars plus $1 for each additional book if ordering from Canada. New York State residents must add sales tax.

To see our complete catalog on the World Wide Web, or to order online, you can find us at *www.allworth.com*.